Paul A. Crony

8 —

# LIVING TRADITION

# LIVING TRADITION

## Orthodox Witness
## in the
## Contemporary World

John Meyendorff

ST. VLADIMIR'S SEMINARY PRESS
CRESTWOOD, NY 10707
1978

Library of Congress Cataloging in Publication Data

Meyendorff, Jean, 1926—
    Living Tradition.

    Includes bibliographical references.
    1.  Theology, Eastern church—Addresses,
essays, lectures.   I.   Title
BX320.2.M475      230'.1'9                        78-2031
    ISBN 0-913836-48-6

ISBN 0-913836-48-6

© 1978
St. Vladimir's Seminary Press

PRINTED IN THE UNITED STATES OF AMERICA
BY
ATHENS PRINTING COMPANY
NEW YORK, N.Y.

# Table of Contents

# Introduction

How is the Orthodox Christian to maintain and witness to his faith in the complicated and changing world of the twentieth century? There can be no answer to this challenge of our age without *living tradition*.

Of necessity, any Orthodox theology and any Orthodox witness is *traditional*, in the sense that it is consistent not only with Scripture but also with the experience of the Fathers and the saints, as well as with the continuous celebration of Christ's death and resurrection in the liturgy of the Church. However the term "traditional theology" can also denote a dead theology, if it means identifying traditionalism with simple repetition. Such a theology may prove incapable of recognizing the issues of its own age, while it presents yesterday's arguments to confront new heresies.

In fact, dead traditionalism cannot be truly traditional. It is an essential characteristic of patristic theology that it was able to face the challenges of its own time while remaining consistent with the original apostolic Orthodox faith. Thus simply to *repeat* what the Fathers said is to be unfaithful to their spirit and to the intention embodied in their theology.

The great Cappadocian Fathers of the fourth century— St. Basil the Great, St. Gregory of Nazianzus, and St. Gregory of Nyssa—are true pillars of Orthodox Christianity because they succeeded in preserving the faith in the face of two great dangers. The first was the Arian heresy, which denied the divinity of Christ, and the second was the influential challenge of ancient Greek philosophy. The latter had ruled the minds of educated people for centuries; and precisely because it appeared as so attractive, so traditional and so prestigious, it prevented many educated Greeks from adopting the new biblical faith of Jesus' disciples. The Fathers faced both of these problems clearly and dealt with them specifically. They did not simply anathematize the Arians but also provided a positive and contemporary terminology to explain the mystery of the Holy Trinity: the terminology enshrined in the Church's creed. They did not simply deny the validity of Greek philosophy but demonstrated as well that its best intuitions could successfully be used in Christian theology, provided one accepted the Gospel of Christ as the ultimate criterion of truth.

Thus for us to be "traditional" implies an imitation of the Fathers in their creative work of discernment. Like them we must be dedicated to the task of saving human beings from error, and not just maintaining abstract propositional truths. We must imitate their constant effort to understand their contemporaries and to use words and concepts which could truly reach the minds of the listeners. True tradition is always a *living* tradition. It changes while remaining always the same. It changes because it faces different situations, not because its essential content is modified. This content is not an abstract proposition; it is the Living Christ Himself, who said, "I am the Truth."

In this last quarter of the twentieth century the Orthodox Church and Orthodox theology find themselves in a very peculiar and divided situation. In Eastern Europe, where most Orthodox Christians live, political conditions are making any expression of living theology very difficult. The Church survives in the limited framework of its liturgical life, which the State tolerates as an outdated museum-piece. Many signs indicate, however, that the spiritual potential of Orthodoxy, preserved primarily in the remarkable dynamism of its worship, remains intact. Moreover the tragic and artificial isolation of the Orthodox communities may one day be recognized as providential. Cutting off Orthodoxy, as the Turkish yoke did in the past, it may well protect it from the temptations and vagaries of contemporary Western secularism.

Quite different is our own situation in the West. No
formal limitations stand in the way of our full intellectual
freedom. This is not to say that we do not face temptations
which are more subtle and in a sense more dangerous than
those of our fellow Orthodox in Eastern Europe. The crisis of
our liturgical tradition, for example, or the canonical chaos in
which we live are clear indications that we fail in using our
God-given freedom to the glory of God.

The task of living theology, expressing the one and living
Tradition of the Church, consists in defining the problems
of our day and giving answers in accordance with the requirements of the one truth of Christ's Gospel. The urgency of
the task is made even more obvious by the fact that non-
Orthodox Christendom, as well as the secular, non-Christian
world, provide us with numerous opportunities for an articulate Orthodox witness. The present book contains several
papers presented by the author at ecumenical gatherings and
dialogue sessions. However there are no grounds for any
Orthodox triumphalism in terms of concrete achievements.
It must be recognized that the participation of the various
Orthodox churches and of numerous Orthodox theologians
in the ecumenical movement during the past decades has not
had any major effect on the development of Western
theology.

All the years of "friendship" between Orthodoxy and
Anglicanism stand as an example. Neither this friendship nor
solemn Orthodox warnings deterred recent developments in
the Protestant Episcopal Church in America. The Episcopalians
approved the ordination of women and also rejected a proposal
(intended as a form of rapprochement with the Orthodox)
to drop the Latin *filioque* addition in their creed. If our Anglican friends are, in their majority, so obviously indifferent to
the traditional Orthodox stand, how can one expect a more
positive position from the broad spectrum of Protestant communities whose representatives we meet at the various ecumenical meetings?

This obvious lack of concern among what one might call
the Western Christian theological and ecclesiastical establishment for the contemporary witness of Orthodoxy sometimes

leads the Orthodox themselves to become quite negative and pessimistic about the Orthodox ecumenical witness. Before succumbing to such pessimism, one, however, should consider a broader and more "catholic" conception of the Church's responsibility in the contemporary world. One need not be limited to the formal structures of the ecumenical movement.

The broader and more "catholic" view of our witness should include the fact that on certain levels, for instance spirituality and ecclesiology, Orthodoxy does exercise a continuing influence which most Orthodox tend themselves to overlook. This influence is possible precisely because, in spite of historic weakness, the Orthodox Church does not follow the advice of moody pessimists and remain alone on the misanthropic shelf of sectarian self-righteousness. Instead she continues to show a measure of humble and compassionate concern for others.

Finally, there is one situation which the Orthodox cannot afford to forget any longer. The major obstacle to Orthodox credibility in the contemporary world lies in the blatant inconsistency between the Orthodox doctrine of the Church and the reality which both Orthodox and non-Orthodox are able to see in the life and organization of the Orthodox churches, particularly in countries of the West. A special chapter of this book deals specifically with this problem and seeks to provide constructive suggestions for ending the ecclesiological chaos, which fortunately is recognized as scandalous by an increasing number of responsible Orthodox churchmen today. Our claim to the "One, Holy, Catholic, and Apostolic Church" in the world in general, and in every country, town, and locality in particular, simply cannot be taken seriously if the traditional canons which express and protect that claim continue to be ignored.

It is our deep belief that the intellectual and spiritual freedom enjoyed by the Orthodox Church in Western countries has been given us by God with a purpose. This purpose consists in making us a permanent workshop of free Orthodox thought and practice, so that the whole of universal Orthodoxy may one day profit from what we do. God puts us to the test, not the test of fire suffered by millions of our brothers in Europe since 1917, but the test of life and of freedom. This is why the problem of "living tradition" is indeed our problem.

In using the title *Living Tradition* for this volume I did not forget that in 1930 a group of eminent Russian émigré theologians in Paris published a collection of articles in Russian under that same title.[1] The impact of the collection was not as strong as it could have been because the Western world was not at that time sufficiently attuned to the authors' witness, and their native country was totally closed to them. In giving the same title to this present book I gladly acknowledge my indebtedness to the spiritual seed they sowed forty years ago.

*—John Meyendorff*

---

[1]*Zhivoe Predanie, Pravoslavie v sovremennosti* (YMCA Press, Paris, n.d.).

# 1
# The Meaning of Tradition

The apostolic *kerygma* proclaimed to the world a historic event which happened "under Pontius Pilate," at a determined date and in a definite setting. This unique event was, on the one hand, the fulfillment of the whole history of the Old Testament. Jesus Christ is "He of whom it was spoken in the law and the prophets" (John 1:45). On the other hand, it was the unique origin of universal salvation for succeeding generations. The essential meaning of the New Testament supposes that Christ's redemptive act has been completed once and for all, that nothing can be added to it, and that there is no other way of benefiting from it but by hearing the word of God proclaimed by the "witnesses." The Church is called "apostolic" by reference to these witnesses, and this adjective is even used in the Creed in order to make plain that link with Christ's immediate disciples.

These fundamental principles must necessarily determine our attitude towards "Scripture" and "Tradition."

## I. Scripture, Tradition, and the Church

Anyone familiar with the Byzantine liturgical ethos, or with any other traditional rites, whether Western or Eastern, knows of the open and solemn *veneration of the Bible* which those rites require.[1] This veneration means more than the solemn

[1]Cf. our essay on "Bible and Tradition in the Orthodox Church," in *The Student World* (Geneva, 1958, no. 1), pp. 39-45.

reading of biblical passages, the constant repetition of verses from the Psalms, and the daily singing of hymns taken from the Old and New Testaments. It obviously means the veneration of Holy Scripture, in particular the Gospel, as a book. This is the meaning of the incensing and kissing of the Gospel, of the processions in which the Holy Book has the place of honor and represents Christ Himself revealed in His Word.

The only possible purpose of this liturgical veneration of Scripture is to suggest to the faithful that it contains the very Truth of Revelation, which the Church possesses precisely in a given written form. It is important to note in this connection that whatever value is attributed to Tradition and to the notion of the Church's continuity in the Truth and her infallibility, the Christian Church never added its own doctrinal definitions to Scripture. Founded upon the apostolic *kerygma*, it included alongside the inspired literature of the Jews the written evidence only of those who had seen the risen Lord with their own eyes and who could write down for the Church the very words of the Master, faithfully interpreting His teaching. The Church had only to define the "canon," not to compose inspired writings, because she never believed in any "continuous revelation," but only in the unique historical act of God, accomplished once and for all in Christ. The writings owed their authority to the fact that they had been composed by the eye witnesses of Christ. The Church could only confirm this authenticity through the guidance of the Spirit promised by Jesus Himself, not create it. This authenticity, of course, is to be understood in a wider sense and as concerning certainly the content, but not necessarily the form of scriptural texts. The gospels of Mark and Luke, for instance, were considered as part of the canon from the very beginning, although they were not composed by members of the college of the Twelve, but the content of their *kerygma* was traditionally attributed to the evidence of Peter and Paul. Origen and other early Christians who doubted the Pauline authenticity of Hebrews did not mean that it should be rejected from the canon, for they did not doubt the fact that it was covered by Pauline authority in a wider sense than direct authorship. No one ever suggested, on the other hand, that anything besides apostolic writings should be included in the canon; and it is this general principle which determined the rejection of the *Shepherd of Hermas* and the *Epistle of Barnabas* from the canon of Scripture.

Apostolicity thus remained the basic criterion in the history of the formation of the canon because it was also the only true characteristic of the Christian *kerygma* as such. The Church's intervention and judgment concerned only the *limits* of true Revelation; and in order to exercise this judgment it needed a criterion external to, but not independent from, Scripture. This criterion is the guidance of the Spirit, through whom the Incarnation was realized and who abides both upon Christ Himself, and upon His Body the Church. The Church, as the community of those who have received the salvation brought by concrete historical events, can have no other foundation than "the apostles and the prophets" (Eph. 2:20) who witnessed to "that which they have heard, which they have seen with their eyes, which their hands have touched" (I John 1:1); but this salvation of which they are witnesses has precisely the result of bringing God to live among us and of making the Spirit "guide us into all Truth" (John 16:3).

We have just said that Scripture contained the entirety of the apostolic witness. This entirety, however, is not a verbal entirety, just as the authenticity of scriptural texts is not necessarily a formal or verbal authenticity. The Word of Life is not a theological encyclopedia which has only to be opened at the right page for the desired information to be found, exhaustively treated. As for instance the works of Oscar Cullmann or Joachim Jeremias have shown, modern exegesis discovers more and more that essential Christian truths, such as the doctrine of the sacraments, not treated directly by the inspired authors, are considered by them as self-evident. Jesus' logia on the Bread of Heaven, the Vine, or "water springing up unto eternal life" (even if the sacramental interpretation of these passages is not the only possible one) cannot be fully understood if one ignores the fact

that Christians in the first century practiced Baptism and performed the Eucharist. This makes it quite clear that Scripture, while complete in itself, presupposes Tradition, not as
an addition, but as a *milieu* in which it becomes understandable and meaningful. At a time when no discussions had
yet occurred on the "number of sources" of Revelation, St.
Basil of Caesarea, in plain and almost naive language, states
the interdependence and essential unity of Scripture and
Tradition in a famous passage of his *Treatise on the Holy
Spirit*: "Among the doctrines and teachings preserved by the
Church, we hold some from written sources, and we have
collected others transmitted in an unexplicit form[2] from
apostolic tradition. They have all the same value... For if
we were to try to put aside the unwritten customs as having
no great force, we should, unknown to ourselves, be weaken-
ning the Gospel in its very essence; furthermore, we should
be transforming the *kerygma* into mere word."[3] He continues by referring specifically to the rites of Christian initia-
tion and the Eucharist.

There cannot be, therefore, any question about "two
sources" of Revelation. It is not in fact a formal dictation
of certain formally definable truths to the human mind.
Revelation in Jesus Christ is a new fellowship between God
and man, established once and for all. It is a participation of man in divine life. Scripture does not create this
participation; it witnesses, in a final and complete form, to
the acts of God which realized it. In order to be fully understood, the Bible requires the reality of the fellowship which
exists in the Church. Tradition is the sacramental continuity
in history of the communion of saints; in a way, it is the
Church itself.

The Orthodox definitely believe in the absolute, organic,
and infallible character of this continuity, and see it as implied by the very nature of Scripture. If the continuity were

----

[2]*Mystikos*: this adverb, which can also mean "secretly" and "sacramen-
tally," seems to be used here in order to imply that certain doctrines were
kept in the closed Christian community, as distinct from the Scriptures,
which were known to all.

[3]*De Spiritu Sancto*, 27.

broken, Scripture would lose its meaning, and that which God wished to do through the Incarnation would in fact have failed. Failures do, of course, occur in individual lives, and in the lives of whole nations and societies; but the Church, as a gift of God, cannot be a failure, "for He wished to present it in splendor, without spot or wrinkle or any such thing, that she might be holy and without blemish" (Eph. 5:27). The existence of this Church is a perfectly free gift of God, and its infallibility is in no sense deserved by those who compose it, but is solely the consequence of the fact that God dwells in her. All members of the Church, every Christian community, may succumb to sin as well to error; but through that very fact they cut themselves off from the Church and must be reunited afresh through penitence.

## II. Tradition and Dogma

While essentially and permanently self-identical, the Church lives in history. The divine Truth which abides in her must, therefore, always face new challenges and be expressed in new ways. The Christian message is not only to be kept unchangeable, but it must also be *understood* by those to whom it is sent by God; it must answer new questions posed by new generations. Thus enters another function of holy Tradition: to make Scripture available and understandable to a changing and imperfect world. In this world, treating problems in isolation from Tradition by simplistic references to Scripture may lead to error and heresy.

The history of doctrinal controversies since the beginning of Christianity shows the evident concern of major theologians and Fathers of the Church to preserve in their teaching not only the meaning of Scripture, but even its wording. This concern did not prevent them, however, from using nonscriptural terms when the defense of the Truth required it. In the fourth century the Nicene Creed was carefully drawn so that only scriptural terms were originally used. It was with the greatest difficulty that Athanasius of Alexandria succeeded in having the word *homoousios* included in order

to express, in a language understandable in his time, a truth
which Scripture presupposed. This example clearly illustrates
the Church's awareness of possessing a living Truth which
cannot be limited by purely biblical wording.

The verbal freedom which the Nicene Fathers demonstrated was not, however, an internal liberty in relation to the
evidence of Scripture. The Orthodox Church has never proclaimed dogmas which are not direct interpretations of historical facts related in the Bible. Let us take a concrete and
still relevant example, that of the veneration of Mary, the
Mother of God. For the Orthodox this veneration rests essentially on the dogma of the anti-Nestorian Council of
Ephesus (431), which in no way made any "Mariological"
definition, but simply condemned a doctrine, attributed to
Nestorius, according to which Christ was a union of two
"subjects": the son of Mary and the Son of God. However,
there was in Christ only one "subject." This was the Son of
God, who became also son of Mary. Therefore Mary must
be the Mother of the Son of God Himself. Thus she is the
"Mother of God," *Theotokos*. It is clear that the council
was essentially concerned with the understanding of an
eminently biblical fact, the Incarnation. In order to express
the full actuality of the Incarnation, we recognize Mary as
the "Mother of God" and not of a simple man, and consequently judge her worthy of quite exceptional veneration.
On the other hand, the doctrine of the Immaculate Conception appears to the Orthodox theologian as not only absent
from the biblical narrative, but also contrary to the biblical
and traditional doctrine of the original sin. In the case of
the Virgin's Assumption and bodily glorification, the tradition is formally preserved in Orthodox liturgical books and
is very widely found in the patristic writings of the Byzantine
Middle Ages. However, a definite uneasiness prevailed
among the Orthodox with the proclamation of the dogma
by Pius XII. The several, partly diverging, traditions which
exist concerning the Assumption seem to them as belonging
to a category of religious facts which essentially differ from
those subject to doctrinal definitions. Although Scripture itself records similar cases, that of Elijah, for instance, the

absence of any reference to the death and glorification of the
Virgin in the Bible seems to indicate clearly that these events
played no essential part in the work of salvation as such.
Consequently there was no need for the Word of God to
recount them and guarantee their authenticity. The entire
Gospel changes in meaning if Christ is not one but two distinct subjects, while it remains strictly the same whether the
Virgin was, or was not, glorified in her very body after her
death. The reserve, expressed almost unanimously by the
Orthodox when the dogma of the Assumption was proclaimed, does not presuppose any *denial* of the corporal
glorification of the Virgin, which is indeed testified by a
fairly ancient tradition, for it certainly appears to be in conformity with the divine plan concerning which God "hath
done great things" (Luke 1:49). But no *theological* necessity seems to justify its inclusion among facts which realized
the salvation of mankind.

These examples were brought forth here not for the sake
of polemics on the issues which they involve, but in order to
illustrate the Orthodox approach to the problem of "doctrinal
development," whose meaning consists neither in a sort of
continuous revelation, nor in making additions to Scripture,
but in solving concrete problems related to the one eternal
Truth, the latter remaining essentially the same before and
after the definition. This attitude is clearly reflected in the
decisions of the early councils. Here is the beginning of the
Chalcedonian definition (451): "The wise and salutary
formula of divine grace[4] *sufficed* for the perfect knowledge
and confirmation of religion ... But, for as much as persons
undertaking to make void the preaching of the truth have
through their individual heresies given rise to empty bab-
blings ..., this present holy, great and ecumenical synod,
desiring to exclude every device against the truth, and teaching that which is unchanged from the beginning, has
decreed ... "[5]

---

[4] The context shows that this "formula" is the Creed of Nicaea-Constantinople.

[5] English text in *Nicene and Post-Nicene Fathers*, second series, vol. 14
(Grand Rapids, Michigan: Eerdmans), p. 203.

Doctrinal definitions are normally made by ecumenical councils, but sometimes also by local councils, or through a simple general *consensus* of the Church. These definitions are final and cannot be changed inasmuch as they express the absolute Truth of Christ, living in His Church. As we have seen earlier, Tradition is but an expression of the permanent presence of God in the community of the New Israel. This presence has its source in God Himself, and does not come from any external criterion or sign. Continuity, permanence, and infallibility come from the fact that in every place and at every time there is "one Lord, one faith, one baptism" (Eph. 4:4-5). No juridical criteria or conditions can replace this presence. This is why Church history knows many "pseudo-councils" (that of 449, for instance) which possessed the signs of ecumenicity, but were finally rejected because they were not in the Truth, and also several councils which were not assembled as ecumenical, but later acquired an ecumenical authority. And, of course, while acknowledging the moral authority of certain local churches, and in particular that of the first among them, the Orthodox Church does not see any ecclesiological or historical reason to recognize in one particular episcopal see a final criterion of Truth.

This lack in Orthodox ecclesiology of a clearly defined, precise, and permanent criterion of Truth besides God Himself, Christ, and the Holy Spirit, is certainly one of the major contrasts between Orthodoxy and all classical Western ecclesiologies. In the West the gradually developed theory of papal infallibility was opposed, after the collapse of the conciliar movement, by the Protestant affirmation of *sola Scriptura*. The entire Western ecclesiological problem since the sixteenth century turned around this opposition of two *criteria*, two references of doctrinal *security*, while in Orthodoxy no need for, or necessity of, such a security was ever really felt for the simple reason that the living Truth is its own criterion. This opposition was rightly emphasized in the nineteenth century by the Russian theologian A. S. Khomiakov, but it is based upon a concept of the Church which was already that of Irenaeus: "Where the Church is, there is the

Spirit of God; and where the Spirit of God is, there is the Church, and every kind of grace; but the Spirit is Truth."[6]

## III. Tradition and Traditions[7]

No clear notion of the true meaning of Tradition can be reached without constantly keeping in mind the well-known condemnation of "human traditions" by the Lord Himself. The one Holy Tradition, which constitutes the self-identity of the Church through the ages and is the organic and visible expression of the life of the Spirit in the Church, is not to be confused with the inevitable, often creative and positive, sometimes sinful, and always relative accumulation of human traditions in the historical Church.

The distinction between "Tradition" and "traditions" is certainly one of the major tasks of the contemporary ecumenical dialogue, and it constitutes one of the most urgent responsibilities of Orthodox theologians. For even outside of its ecumenical involvement, the Orthodox Church faces this problem with a particular acuity.

An Orthodox generally conceives his Christianity as an integral whole which finds its expression in doctrinal convictions as well as in liturgical worship and in whatever attitude he takes as a Christian. This attitude is quite different from that of the average Roman Catholic, who is much more ready to accept change when it comes from the proper authority. Its psychological root is in the absence of an absolute, permanent doctrinal power (noted above) and in the positive sense of *responsibility* that an Orthodox usually has for the *integrity* of his faith. He is, consciously or unconsciously, but rightly, aware of the fact that all acts of worship have some doctrinal implications and that true Christianity is to be taken as a whole set of beliefs and attitudes. At an elementary level, when he is not able to make the necessary

[6]*Adversus haereses* III, 24, 1; English translation in *The Ante-Nicene Fathers* I (New York, 1925), p. 458.

[7]Cf. our essay under this title in *St. Vladimir's Theological Quarterly* vol. 6 (1962), pp. 118-127.

distinctions between the essential and the secondary, he prefers to preserve *everything.* The formal and ritualistic conservatism of Eastern Christians undoubtedly played a positive role in history. It helped them to preserve their faith during the dark ages of the Mongolian and Turkish occupations. However, it does not reflect as such the catholicity of the Church. Today, it represents a problem which Orthodox theologians have to handle if they want to face seriously not only the modern world and the ecumenical movement, but also a number of reformist movements inside the Orthodox world itself. The first task of Orthodox theology today must be to rediscover, through a true sense of catholicity, the role of the one, holy Tradition of the Church, as distinct from the pseudo-absolute and human traditions. If one turns to the past of the Church, it is surprising how many traditional authorities one can find to support this rediscovery, especially in documents related to the schism between East and West.

Since apostolic times Christians have always conceived their unity as unity in faith, although it was obvious that every local church could express this faith in its own language, liturgical rite, and, originally, even in its own baptismal creed. This linguistic and liturgical variety did not at all prevent church unity from remaining a very practical reality. In the second century Irenaeus could speak of a unique apostolic Tradition equally well preserved in Rome, Smyrna, and Ephesus. When Christological controversies broke the unity of the Eastern Church, the situation began to change. The schism roughly followed existing cultural and linguistic boundaries, and a majority of non-Greek Eastern Christians (Copts, Syrians, Armenians, Ethiopians) adopted monophysitic confessions of faith. The Orthodox Chalcedonian churches followed Rome and Constantinople, and their influence was practically restricted to the Graeco-Latin world of the Roman Empire. Finally, this unity was itself broken with the great schism between the Ancient and the New Rome, again following racial and linguistic lines.

The prestige of these two centers was so great in their respective areas that all non-Roman and non-Constantinopolitan traditions tended to disappear during a long process of evolution lasting from the sixth to the twelfth century. Both sides started to recognize the ethos and practices of their respective metropolis as the only acceptable pattern. In the East the ancient Egyptian, Syrian, and Palestinian liturgies were gradually replaced in the Orthodox Church by the Byzantine rite. In the eleventh century Patriarch Michael Cerularius, in his attacks against the Latins, was already firmly convinced that the practices accepted in the "city guarded by God," i.e. Constantinople, constituted the only true Christian tradition. For him there was no longer any distinction between *the* Tradition of the Church and the local practices of the imperial capital.[8] His Latin opponents adopted an even sharper attitude in their famous decree of excommunication against Michael, deposited on July 16, 1054, on the altar of St. Sophia.[9] The extreme point of the controversy was reached when Pope Innocent III, after the conquest of Constantinople by the Crusaders in 1204, thought for a brief time that it was possible to realize an integrally Latin Christendom under his leadership.[10]

Fortunately the Orthodox Church has always found in its midst a number of eminent witnesses faithful to the ancient catholic Tradition. The process of liturgical unification according to the practice of the Great Church of Constantinople did not prevent the translation of the Byzantine rite into the language of the various peoples converted to Orthodoxy. In fact it was the use of the vernacular as the liturgical language that gave the Byzantine missionaries their principal element of success throughout the Middle Ages. It prevented the Greek Church from undergoing a fossilization comparable to that of the Nestorian and Monophysite churches in the Middle East.

On the other hand, the great Byzantine theologians were always conscious of the necessary distinction between "Tradi-

[8]See especially his letter to Peter of Antioch, in Migne, P.G. 120, cols. 781-796.

[9]Text in Migne, P.L. 147, col. 1004.

[10]In his letters of that time, the Pope speaks of maintaining the Greek liturgy and practices in Constantinople only as a temporary tolerance (Migne, P.L. 216, col. 902; 215, col. 964D-965A); cf. O. Rousseau, "La question

tion" and "traditions." In the very midst of the Graeco-Latin disputes about rites and practices several voices were heard restoring the true scale of values, and it is good to keep their memory alive today.

Patriarch Photius is the first to be mentioned here. Condemned by Pope Nicholas I on the basis of canonical norms unknown in the East, Photius proclaimed the principle of coexistence in the universal Church of all legitimate local traditions: "Everybody must preserve what was defined by common ecumenical decisions," he writes to Nicholas, "but a particiular opinion of a church father, or a definition issued by a local council, can be followed by some and ignored by others. Thus, some people customarily shave their beards, others reject this practice through (local) conciliar decrees. Thus, as far as we are concerned, we consider it reprehensible to fast on Saturdays, except once a year (on Holy Saturday), while others fast on other Saturdays as well. Thus Tradition avoids disputes by making practice prevail over the rule. In Rome, there are no priests legitimately married, while our tradition permits men once married to be elevated to the priesthood . . ." Photius alludes here to the legislation of the council *in Trullo*, or Quinisext (691), which Rome did not receive. He consciously avoids imposing it upon the Westerners and finally establishes a general principle: "When the faith remains inviolate, the common and catholic decisions are also safe; a sensible man respects the practices and laws of others; he considers that it is neither wrong to observe them, nor illegal to violate them."[11] Faith alone, according to Photius, is thus the criterion for judging the practices of the local churches; nothing else can be opposed to their legitimate variety.[12]

Similar to that of Photius was the attitude of Peter, Patri-

des rites entre Grecs et Latins des premiers siècles au concile de Florence," *Irénikon* vol. 22 (149), pp. 253-254; M. Jugie, *Le schisme byzantin* (Paris, 1941), p. 253.

[11]*Ep.* 2, in Migne, P.G. 102, cols. 604D-605D.

[12]In his encyclical of 867, Photius resorted to purely disciplinary and liturgical accusations against the Latins (Saturday fasting, sacerdotal celibacy, chrismation administered by bishops alone), but he had in view the Latin missionary activity in Bulgaria, an area which he considered as part of his

arch of Antioch and correspondent of Michael Cerularius.
He gave Michael the advice to restrict his criticism of the
Latins to the doctrinal question of the *filioque* and to con-
sider the other standing points of litigation as "indifferent."[13]
A contemporary, Theophylact, Greek archbishop of Ochrid,
in a treatise consecrated to Graeco-Latin polemics, also considers the question of the procession of the Holy Spirit as
the only serious problem between Constantinople and Rome.
Setting aside the liturgical and canonical accusations of
Cerularius, he returns to the principle defined by Photius:
"Unless one ignores ecclesiastical history, one will not use
such arguments; only those practices can threaten church
unity which have a doctrinal implication."[14]

   In the fourteenth and the fifteenth centuries all contacts
between Greeks and Latins implicitly presupposed, at least
in Byzantine minds, that reunified Christendom would preserve a variety of local traditions. Nicholas Cabasilas, in
speaking of the *epiclesis* of the Spirit at the Eucharist, re-
calls the Latin rite itself as an argument in favor of the
Byzantine position;[15] there is no doubt that for him the Latin
liturgical tradition possesses a catholic authenticity.

   In modern times this attitude has become practically
universal. In 1895, for instance, the Ecumenical Patriarch
Anthimos and his synod expressed it in their reply to the
encyclical *Praeclara gratulationis* of Pope Leo XIII; the union
of the churches can be realized through unity of faith, but
this unity does not imply a unification of "the order of the
holy services, hymns, liturgical vestments and other similar
things which, even when they preserve their former variety,
do not endanger the essence and unity of the faith."[16]

   The establishment of a clear distinction between the holy
"Tradition" as such, and the human traditions created by

patriarchate and where Latin clergy were denying the validity of Greek practices. There is therefore no essential contradiction between his attitude in
861 and 867.
   [13]Migne, P.G. 120, cols. 812A-813A.
   [14]Migne, P.G. 126, col. 245B.
   [15]*Explanation of the Divine Liturgy*, XXX; trans. by J. M. Hussey and
McNulty (London: SPCK, 1960).
   [16]I. N. Karmires, *Ta dogmatika kai symbolika mnemeia tes orthodoxou
katholikes ekklesias*, vol. II (Athens, 1953), p. 935.

history, is probably the most essential aspect of contemporary
theology, especially when and if it wants to be ecumenical.
The very reality of Tradition, a living and organic reality
manifesting the presence of the Spirit in the Church and
therefore also its *unity*, cannot be fully understood unless it
is clearly distinguished from everything which creates a normal *diversity* inside the one Church. To disengage Holy
Tradition from the human traditions which tend to monop-
olize it is in fact a necessary condition of its preservation, for
once it becomes petrified into the forms of a particular culture, it not only excludes the others and betrays the catholicity
of the Church, but it also identifies itself with a passing and
relative reality and is in danger of disappearing with it.

Therein lies a very urgent problem for contemporary
Orthodoxy, especially in connection with its ecumenical responsibility and involvement. There was a time when the
"Christian East" as such stirred enthusiasm in ecumenical
circles as a beautiful, exotic, and mysterious tradition, attractive because it was "different." With the growth of
mutual knowledge and information this phase now belongs
to the past, simply because the ecumenical movement has
been taken seriously by its participants. While still apprecia-
tive of the possible contributions which could be made by
local traditions to the catholic reality of the *Una Sancta*, they
look forward to the *One Church* itself. The *union of all* is
the fundamental aim of ecumenical activity and thought. The
obvious Orthodox responsibility is to show *where* this union
can become a reality and *how* it can be realized. The claim
of the Orthodox Church to be already the *Una Sancta* must
be substantiated in the empirical reality of its life, so that
it may really appear also as the *Catholica*. This is precisely
the goal of the internal reformation which the Roman
Church is seeking presently in order to substantiate her own
similar claim.

But all these efforts will bring forth fruit only if they
end upon an *encounter*, not only with each other, but also
with the Lord in the Spirit of Truth. To be truly "ecumenical"
is to be ready at every moment for this encounter, which will
come on a day and at an hour when we least expect it.

# 2

# Historical Relativism and Authority in Christian Dogma*

"The Church is not an authority, just as God is not an authority and Christ is not an authority, since authority is something external to us. The Church is not authority, I say, but the Truth—and at the same time the inner life of the Christian, since God, Christ, the Church live in him with a life more real than the heart which is beating in his breast and the blood flowing in his veins. But they are alive in him only insofar as he himself is living by the ecumenical life of love and unity; i.e., by the life of the Church." This categorical statement by A. S. Khomiakov, a Russian lay theologian and publicist of the last century whose lasting influence has not vanished among contemporary Orthodox theologians, is only an introduction to his sweeping definition of the ultimate difference between Orthodoxy on the one hand, and the whole of Western Christianity on the other, as a conflict over "authority" in religion. In the West, according to Khomiakov, "authority became external power," and "knowledge of religious truths [was] cut off from religious life." Church authority bestowed these truths upon human *reason* alone as means "necessary" or "useful" for salvation; and in the Reformation the external authority of the Church was replaced by that of Scripture. In both cases, Khomiakov writes, "the premises are identical."[1]

___

*Paper delivered at a meeting of the American Theological Society on March 31, 1967, and published originally in *St. Vladimir's Theological Quarterly* vol. 11:2 (1967), pp. 73-86.

[1]The quotations are taken from A. S. Khomiakov's famous French pamphlet:

The essential merit of these polemical overstatements is to illustrate the fact that the problem of authority has a long history, especially in East-West relations, and that it involves not only the question *what* or *who* possesses authority, but also a definition of the very concept of authority in matters pertaining to the Christian faith. This preliminary question must be kept in mind throughout our entire discussion of authority.

### I. The Authority of God

The absolute authority of God is one of the basic ideas of the Old Testament. The revelation of His will is itself an expression of His mercy and can be received only with "fear and trembling."[2] Thus the Covenant at Sinai is understood as an exclusively divine initiative, and Israel is constantly reminded by the prophets of Yahweh's *right* to impose His conditions. One of the main topics of the prophetic preaching is, in fact, to dispel the view that Yahweh has any need of Israel and that the Covenant has any similarity with a bargain-type agreement. This one-sidedness of the Covenant has been expressed in the use of the Greek διαθήκη ("testament" or "will") by the Septuagint to translate the Hebrew *b'rith*, instead of an expression like συνθήκη, which would interpret the Covenant as a bilateral pact. It is by this unilateral obedience to God's commandments that Israel will fulfill her terms of the agreement and then receive God's protection and guidance. "You have declared this day concerning the Lord that He is your God, and that you will walk in His ways, and keep His statutes and His commandments and His ordinances, and will obey His voice; and the Lord

---

*Quelques mots d'un chrétien orthodoxe sur les confessions occidentales* (Paris, 1853), reprinted in *L'Eglise latine et le protestantisme au point de vue de l'Eglise d'Orient. Recueil d'articles sur des questions religieuses ecrits à différentes époques et à différentes occasions* (Lausanne and Vevey, 1872), pp. 36-37. A convenient English translation by A. E. Morehouse is now available in A. Schmemann, ed., *Ultimate Questions* (New York: Holt, Rinehart and Winston, 1965), pp. 50-51.

[2]Classical passages are Gen. 18:27; Ex. 3:6; Is. 6:4-5; Job 42:2-3.

has declared this day concerning you that you are a people for His own possession, as He has promised you, and that you are to keep all His commandments" (Dt. 27:17-18).

The Old Testament idea of covenant reflects the very limit of God's authority, an external authority often expressed in the anthropomorphic categories of monarchy, absolute and fear-inspiring. And we know that Paul starts precisely with that idea to explain in Romans the content of the Christian *kerygma*: "He has mercy upon whomever He wills, and He hardens the heart of whomever He wills... Who are you, man, to answer back to God?" (9:18-20).

However, the New Testament also contains the announcement of a New Covenant which radically changes God's exercise of His authority over men. One of the most striking differences, pointed out by C. H. Dodd, is that the Old Testament "story is about a community; the interpretation comes through individual insight. In the New Testament the story is no longer, primarily, about a community, but about a Person."[3] A personal Messiah assumes the destinies of Israel and becomes a party, on behalf of all humanity, of a New Covenant with God. Moreover, gathering Israel at the foot of Sinai, Moses threw upon it the blood of oxen, as "blood of the covenant" (Ex: 24-8), but Jesus' New Covenant is "in His blood" (I Cor. 11:25, Luke 22:20); or according to Matthew and Mark, Christ's own blood becomes "the blood of the Covenant" (Mt. 26:28, Mk. 14-24).[4]

If, as C. H. Dodd saw, the New Testament speaks of the people of God only "secondarily and derivatively," it is because Israel in the New Covenant becomes the "body" of the Messiah and thus loses its autonomy. In a sense it ceases to be simply a "party" of the agreement with God. The Pauline concept of the Church as "Body of Christ" is, in fact, an assumption of the deutero-Isaian theme of the suffering servant without being a solution of Isaiah's fundamental ambiguity. The Messiah, for Paul, is certainly Jesus; but it is also "in Jesus" the entire New Israel, just as for

[3]*The Bible Today* (Cambridge: Cambridge University Press, 1946), p. 73.

[4]Joachim Jeremias, *The Eucharistic Words of Jesus* (Oxford: Blackwell, 1955), p. 134, note 4.

deutero-Isaiah the image of the servant suggests both a person and Israel as a nation.

The New Covenant, however, implies also a commandment of God; it is the "new commandment" of love (Jn. 13:34), a requirement radically different from that of the Mosaic Law for it represents a personal and mutual relationship. "He who has my commandments and keeps them, he it is who loves me; and he who loves me will be loved by my Father, and I will love him and manifest myself to him" (Jn. 14:21). In both the Pauline and the Johannine understanding of the New Covenant there is in Jesus personal and direct encounter between God and man, an encounter which became accessible to "many" through the mystery of the Resurrection and the presence of the Spirit, an encounter which transcends and replaces the legal and external categories of "commandment-obedience-faithfulness" of the Law.

These basic and well-known themes of the New Testament have a decisive importance for the understanding of authority in the Christian Church, for God is not simply *speaking* to the community any more, while remaining essentially external to it. He is *present* through the Spirit in the community; and the community itself is a community of "saints," of adopted "sons," of freely loving persons who have all received "the seal of the Spirit" (Eph. 1:13) and are "taught by the Spirit" (I Cor. 2:13). "He has put His seal upon us," writes Paul, "and given us His Spirit in our hearts as a guarantee (ἀρραβὼν)" (II Cor. 1:22). The community is the "body," i.e. the very reality of Christ.

The kingly and messianic "authority" (ἐξουσία) of Jesus is stressed throughout the New Testament. The authority to remit sins particularly (Mk. 2:10 par.) is understood as one of the obvious signs of His divinity. This authority, just like that of God the Old Testament lawgiver, requires His people to observe "His commandments" (cf. especially, Mt. 28:20); but the entire character of the commandments is changed and interiorized, as is best shown in Matthew's Sermon on the Mount. Now "all the law and all the prophets" depend upon the commandment of love (Mt. 22:35-40) and, therefore, lose their external and legal character.

What follows from this is that the particular authority commissioned by Jesus to some of His disciples (to Peter, the Twelve, or a larger group) can only be an authority *within* the community, and not *over* it. This is why the exegetes will never stop discussing the problem of defining whether texts like John 20:22 and Matthew 16:18 were addressed to the community or to a narrower group of disciples. Obviously the editors of Jesus' sayings did not feel that this was an issue at all. The identification between Christ and the community made impossible any human authority *over* the People of God. It made necessary, however, an internal structure based upon the sacramental nature of the Church, which soon led, organically and without any dissent, to the generalization of a "monarchical episcopate."[5] Meanwhile, *prophecy*, which had expressed so vividly the authority of God over the people, receives in Pauline ecclesiology nothing but a subsidiary function (I Cor. 14).

However, there is one dimension where human authority stands, in a sense, *above* the Church as a condition of the Church's very existence: the function of being *witness* to Christ's resurrection, assigned by Jesus Himself to a group of disciples "chosen" by Him and, in particular, to the Twelve. "You shall receive power (δύναμιν) when the Holy Spirit has come upon you; and you shall be my witnesses in all Judea and Samaria and to the end of the earth" (Acts 1:8, cf. Luke 24:48, etc.). No Church is possible without faith, but "how are they to believe in Him of whom they have never heard? And how are they to hear without a preacher? And how can men preach unless they are sent (ἀποσταλῶσιν)?" (Rom. 10:14).

Inasmuch as the Christian faith is based upon a historical fact, it relies upon the apostolic "witness," a unique and untransmissible privilege of those who have actually seen the risen Lord. The election of Matthias to replace Judas shows clearly that membership in the college of the Twelve supposed that one was a "witness to His resurrection" (Acts

---

[5]We have dealt more in detail with the connection Church-Eucharist-Bishop in *Orthodoxy and Catholicity* (New York: Sheed and Ward, 1966), pp. 1-16.

1:22). The Church, established and confirmed by the Pentecost event (Acts 2), was therefore both on the authority of the "witnesses" and the guidance of the Spirit. Actually, these authorities presupposed each other. It was inconceivable to have the Spirit contradict the apostolic witness, or to have the apostolic witness delivered outside the framework of the Spirit's activity in the community. The somewhat contradictory missions of Peter and James on the one hand, and of Paul on the other, were conducted not only in their personal names, but also in the names of the churches of Jerusalem and Antioch respectively.

This original *polarity* in early Christian ecclesiology between the personal authority of the apostles and the authority of the Spirit guiding the community provides the possibility of establishing a continuity between the apostolic and the post-apostolic ages. The continuity lies, of course, in the community, and not in the personal witness.

It is symptomatic that the death of one of the Twelve, recorded in Acts, "Herod . . . killed James the brother of John with the sword" (12:2), is not followed by any new election. Judas the apostate needed a substitute, but not James the martyr. As "college" the Twelve ceased to exist historically after James' death, and soon its entire membership was to disappear. The task of the community then would consist in preserving the apostolic message in its original purity and in continuing the missionary and pastoral ministry without them. This became possible not so much because of personal commissions given to individual successors by individual apostles, even if such commissions were occasionally made (cf. Pastoral Epistles), but because of the *sacramental identity* between the Church in Jerusalem, which received the Spirit on the day of Pentecost, and any Church gathered anywhere in the name of Christ.

Thus, the earliest form of the doctrine of Apostolic Succession, as represented by Irenaeus, is actually a doctrine of "Apostolic Tradition." The true *kerygma* of the apostles is preserved not magically, through an imposition of hands by one individual upon another, but through the continuity of the same episcopal office in each community. Not denying the necessity of the imposition of hands, which since the earliest days of the Church was the sign of the gifts of the Spirit and which certainly existed in his time, Irenaeus envisages the episcopate as expressing the *nature of the community*, not as a power or an authority *over* the Church. The "certain *charisma* of truth" possessed by the bishops according to Irenaeus (*Adv. haer.*, IV, 40, 2) is not a personal infallibility, but an expression of the fact that in the Church everything occurs within the sacramental framework of the eucharistic assembly whose president, the bishop, is an image of the Lord and is called to express the will of God. Therefore, again according to St. Irenaeus, "all who wish to see the truth can contemplate the Tradition of the apostles manifested throughout the world in every church" (*Adversus haereses*, III, 31).[6]

Theologically the continuity between the New Testament notion of authority and that of the early Church can therefore be established on the basis of the *sacramental* identity of the Church. Because of the very nature of the New Covenant, God's presence among His people and in the world can no longer be understood either legally or vicariously. The Spirit makes the community to be the Body of the Messiah, and inside this Body God not only speaks *to* men, but He also makes men to speak out His will: "We are God's fellow workers (συνεργοὶ Θεοῦ)" (I Cor. 3:9). The presence of God in the community is what the New Testament generally calls "Spirit," and Paul, sometimes, μυστήριον.

Sacramental life, especially the Eucharist, requires the Church to be internally structured and hierarchical. Inversely, this structure can have a theological foundation only *in* the sacrament, i.e. in the concrete reality of the sacramental local community which is called by Ignatius the "catholic church." There is no theological foundation for any external supreme authority *over* the local sacramental communities, each of whom is the Body of Christ in its totality.

[6]We have discussed the issue more at length in *Orthodoxy and Catholicity*, pp. 18-23.

## II. *Authority and Tradition*

The fact of the continuity of the Church in the Spirit from Pentecost onwards is the key to an acceptable understanding of "Tradition" and its "authority." The gap between the "historical Jesus" and the "faith of the early Church," on which modern form criticism is often based, cannot be considered as simply a gap between "history" and "myth" precisely because there is no other way to "Jesus" except through the faith of the community, whether the "Jesus-event" is historical or not. Innumerable passages of the New Testament point to the fact that the disciples understood who Jesus was only through the community fellowship in the Spirit, for the Spirit "guided them in all truth" (John 16:13). However, it was this new and fuller understanding of Jesus which led the evangelists to write their records and even to go beyond mere reminiscences in order to give "a living representation of all that He had once spoken to His disciples, a creative exposition of the Gospel."[7] It was not a fabric of sayings of Jesus produced to meet the "needs of the *kerygma*." Could one imagine a greater "need" for a decisive "saying" than the dramatic clash over the mission to the Gentiles, reflected in Galatians and Acts? However, neither side made use of Jesus' sayings on the matter precisely because there were none, and nobody proceeded to invent any.[8] The Jerusalem assembly simply formulated what "has seemed good to the Holy Spirit and to us" (Acts 15:28).

The Christian notion of Tradition thus implies both a responsible freedom of the Church to discern the will of God with the Spirit being the only true "security," and a total faithfulness to the oral or written witness of the apostles to Jesus Christ as a historical person. Both of these attitudes require acceptance of the faith of the early community, and this acceptance is that in which the Christian commitment itself consists. The problem of "historical relativism" con-

[7]Edwyn C. Hoskyns, *The Fourth Gospel* (London: Faber and Faber, 1947), p. 485.

[8]Cf. Veselin Kesich, "Criticism, the Gospel and the Church," *St. Vladimir's Seminary Quarterly* vol. 10:3 (1966), pp. 144-145.

cerns, therefore, not only the events of Jesus' life, His Messianic consciousness, the meaning of His sayings, but, first of all, the claim of the early Church to be guided by the Spirit. There can certainly be wide variety in the interpretations of what this guidance implied, but the acknowledgment or denial of its existence is what makes the difference between a Christian and a non-Christian historian. For the faith of the early Church, as it follows from the entire body of the New Testament canon compiled in connection with several crises of interpretation, contains elements historically uncontrollable.[9] While opposed to other interpretations such as the Judaeo-Christian and especially the gnostic, it integrates some of their valid elements. The historian will disentangle the history and respective influences of those early tendencies of exegesis and acknowledge what is or is not scientifically controllable, but his own fundamental theological conviction will depend upon his acceptance or his rejection of the authority of the Spirit acting in the early community. Historical criticism alone will never be able to ascertain who Jesus was.

What we have said previously about the nature of the New Covenant and about the sacraments as the element of continuity and identity in the Church implies that the most basic options (in favor of the mission to the pagans and against gnosticism) taken by the early Church were taken under no other authority than that of the Spirit. However, the guidance of the Spirit is not equivalent with individualism, emotionalism, or anarchy. "Order" was always one of the major concerns of St. Paul (cf. I Cor. 14:40), an order expressing the very nature of the Christian community. It is this "order," based upon the sacramental nature of the Church, which was expressed in the universal adoption of the "monarchical episcopate." The local eucharistic community is the Body of Christ; its president is the image of the Lord Himself and is responsible for the right teaching as well as for the pastoral guidance of the community.

However, precisely because his function derives not from a personal legal "delegation" given to him individually by

---

[9]Cf. a good discussion of this issue in O. Cullmann's latest book, *Le salut dans l'histoire* (Neuchatel: Delachaux et Niestle, 1966), pp. 143 ff.

Christ, but from the action of the Spirit upon the entire community, the bishop cannot possess personal infallibility. His
teachings and opinions must be checked and compared with
those of his colleagues elsewhere. The unity which can be
observed in the teaching of all bishops everywhere is the
main argument in favor of the true "Apostolic Tradition"
given by St. Irenaeus in *Adv. haer.* III. A regional consensus
is therefore a more authoritative sign of Truth than the
opinion of one bishop, and a universal consensus is the
highest authority in matters of faith.

The ecclesiology is the foundation of an institution which
will regulate the life of the Christian Church for many centuries, the councils.

The following remarks on the nature of councils seem
to have a particular importance for our analysis of "authority" in the Church:

(1)   The councils were gatherings of bishops convened
to meet a specific problem of church life (consecration of
new bishops for vacant sees and discussion of doctrinal or
disciplinary issues) and were not a permanent or institutionalized power over the Church. This original function of
the councils is obviously different from the conceptions of
Western "conciliarists" of the fifteenth century, who conceived the council as a ruling committee supplanting and
replacing the Pope. The original council, however, fell essentially in the biblical category of "witness." Agreement on
a given issue was considered to be a *sign* of the will of God,
to be received by the Church with discernment and to be
tested against other "signs": Scripture, Tradition, other councils.

(2)   The councils were not governed by majority rule on
major issues.[10] The minority either had to agree with the
decisions, or face excommunication. This was not simple "in-
tolerance," but a conviction that the Spirit *was* guiding the
Church, and that opposition to the Spirit was incompatible
with church membership.

---

[10]The principle of majority rule was, however, adopted on minor or disciplinary issues in the post-Constantinian period, when the ties established
with the state required elements of legalism in church administration.

(3) The absence of legal guarantees for securing "minority rights" in conciliar decisions did not mean that the majority was infallible *ex sese*. History knows numerable "pseudo-councils," later rejected by the Church, when she endorsed the view of the condemned minority, or even of isolated witnesses to the truth. The case of Athanasius or that of Maximus the Confessor are good examples of this. A conciliar decree needed the "reception" of the whole Church to be considered a true expression of Tradition. This "reception," however, was not a popular referendum or an expression of lay "democracy" as opposed to clerical "aristocracy." It simply implied that no authority suppresses man's freedom to believe or not to believe. Any conciliar decree itself implied the *risk of faith*, and it was not supposed to suppress this risk in others. The Council of Chalcedon was never "received" by large bodies of Eastern Christians. Both the Chalcedonians and the Non-Chalcedonians took the "risk" of schism in the name of what, for them, was the Christian Truth. "Reception" of a council is not to be understood in legal categories. It simply adds to the authority of the conciliar "sign," and also implies the fact that the only ultimate authority in the Christian Church is the Spirit itself.

(4) Alliance with the Roman Empire implied cooperation between a state governed by law and a Church whose internal structure was not legalistic, but sacramental. The state thus constantly tended to force the Church to express itself in legal terms understandable to the Roman authority. Gradually, purely legal elements began to penetrate both the procedure and the decisions of the councils. However, on the most basic issue, that of the faith, the emperors never succeeded in making the early Church express itself with a legal precision and regularity similar to that of the Roman Senate. However, in the eyes of the state the "ecumenical councils" were supposed to fulfill precisely that function: to provide the emperor with a clear formula of faith which was then given legal and binding force by imperial confirmation. In fact, the consciousness of the Church never fully assimilated the procedure. Councils *were* rejected in spite of imperial confirmations, and what we now call "doctrinal de-

velopment" continued to be an organic process in which historical, political, social, or cultural elements played a role, but where the Spirit remained as the only recognized ultimate authority.

(5) The true nature of "doctrinal development" is clearly shown in the decisions of those councils which were finally acknowledged as "ecumenical." Never did any council claim to promote a "new dogma." On the contrary, each affirmed that its decrees were not different from previous definitions (cf., for example, canon 7 of Ephesus, 331). The Fathers of Chalcedon in the preamble to their famous definition proclaim that the Nicene Creed "is sufficient for the perfect knowledge and confirmation of piety, for it teaches the perfect doctrine concerning Father, Son and Holy Spirit, and sets forth the Incarnation of the Lord." The new definition is necessary only because "some persons" undertake "to make void the preaching of the truth through their individual heresies." In other words, doctrinal definition is viewed only as an extraordinary and extreme measure, an antidote to heresy, and not as an end in itself. It is therefore distinct from truth, which is "apostolic," i.e. present explicitly or implicitly in the consciousness of the Church from apostolic times and based upon apostolic witness.

All this indicates that authority in the Church neither suppresses nor diminishes freedom. It rather appeals to it by affirming the faithfulness of God to His New Covenant with man and by proclaiming that, according to the terms of this covenant, God is indeed constantly present in the Church. His sacramental presence involves also His presence in Truth, and the baptismal encounter with new life makes possible and accessible true participation in God. The Christian notion of authority excludes blind obedience and presupposes free and responsible participation of all in the common life of the Body. The sacramental nature of the Body defines, however, a variety of ministries. The episcopate in particular is in charge of defining the historical continuity and consistency of the Christian Gospel ("Tradition"), as well as the horizontal universal communion of all in one Church ("unity of faith" and sacramental communion).

### III. *Anthropological Dimension of Freedom*

To be "called to freedom" (Gal. 5:13) is, for St. Paul, the greatest privilege of Christians. It implies, however, that one is "led by the Spirit" (Gal. 5:18). The idea that the Spirit and freedom do not contradict, but presuppose each other, is connected with the notion of "participation" in God's life, which we have just described as a necessary corollary to the Christian notion of authority. This connection is especially evident in Greek patristic literature.

Already Irenaeus, a trichotomist, saw man as composed of flesh, soul, and *Holy Spirit* (cf., for example, *Adversus haereses* V, 9, 1). This view, which sounds strangely pantheistic if considered in later theological categories, in fact shows a dynamic concept of man which excludes the static notion of "pure nature." Man is created in order to share in God's existence; this is what makes him different from animals. The biblical account of Adam's creation in "God's image" expresses this idea. The Greek patristic doctrine of the "deification" (θέωσις) of man uses Platonic philosophical terminology to convey the same idea. It also implies that neither God's nature nor human nature is "closed" in itself. If God is always seen as totally transcendent and His nature totally "different," so that even the categories of being or existence are inapplicable to Him in the way that they are applicable to creatures, He is also conceived as freely communicating to man what belongs properly to Himself, His own life. Furthermore, man was created precisely as a receptacle of this divine life, without which he ceases to be truly man. It is when he affirms himself as an "autonomous" being and confines himself to "secular" life that he loses not only an extrinsic "grace" or "religion," but his own true existence as man. Original sin does not imply simply an external punishment of man, the deprivation of "supernatural" grace, but a corruption of man who, as man, abandons his own destiny and purpose.

These basic anthropological presuppositions are essential

---

[11]*On the Creation of Man*, XVI, P.G. 44:184B.

for the understanding of freedom and authority in the Church.

Freedom is, for Gregory of Nyssa[11] and Maximus the Confessor,[12] the essential element of man's likeness to God. Freedom, i.e. "to be undetermined," is the most basic of *divine* attributes; but man possesses it by "participation." However, his revolt against God deprived him of freedom, made him a slave to the "flesh," i.e. to the determinism of created existence. Man became a part of *this* world, subject to cosmic laws and especially to corruption, death, and sin.

Now the purpose of the Incarnation is to restore man in his former dignity and, therefore, make him free again. The very difference between the man "in Christ" and the "old Adam" is that the former is *free*. This freedom comes to him not as a legal emancipation, which would leave him to an autonomous existence, but as a share in the dignity of his Creator, a new life in which freedom does not stand by itself, but is the consequence of full knowledge, full vision, and full and positive experience of divine love, truth, and beauty. "You will know the truth, and the truth will make you free" (Jn. 8:32).

The notion of authority in the Church is therefore understandable only in the context of the Pauline opposition between the "first man" and the "last Adam" (I Cor. 15:45 ff.). Authority, like law, is obviously needed only as long as man lives in the "flesh and blood." The problem amounts ultimately to a question about the Church. Is it a society where fallen man, through discipline and obedience to an authority vicariously replacing God, is prevented from being swept into the temptations of the "world," or is it rather the place where he experiences, at least partially, the glorious liberty of the children of God (Rom. 8:21) by contemplating personally and really the Truth itself, by participating in it and thus becoming a witness of the Kingdom *before* the world and *in* the world? It is the second alternative that A. S. Khomiakov wanted to stress when he affirmed that "the Church is not an authority."

[12]*Amb.* 42, P.G. 91:1316D.

## IV. *Authority and History*

The role of the Church is not, therefore, to impose upon man's mind some truth which otherwise he is unable to perceive, *but to make him live and grow in the Spirit, so that he himself may see and experience the Truth.* Hence the negative character of the doctrinal definitions made by the ancient councils. Actually, as we have seen, these definitions never consisted in systematic descriptions of the Truth, but rather in condemnations of erroneous beliefs. The councils never claimed to identify the entire living Truth with their definitions. Indeed, any doctrinal formula and any scriptural text is conditioned by *history*, i.e. by human existence in the fallen world in the midst of limited intellectual, philosophical, or social categories. To absolutize those categories would mean to reduce man to historic determinism, from which the Incarnation liberates him. Doctrinal "development" does not mean enrichment of the original apostolic witness with new revelations, but it implies freedom *from* all particular historical problematics and, conversely, the possibility of expressing the Christian message in *any* historical situation.

Church history knows deliberate use by church "authority" of contemporary philosophical terms in order to express the meaning of the faith. The case of the Nicene *homoousios* is the most famous one and also the most characteristic because the term was previously considered as suspect and even condemned as modalistic in Antioch in 261. There are other historical examples when previous doctrinal statements received new qualifications required by the needs of church unity. The efforts of Emperor Justinian to make the Chalcedonian formula acceptable to the Monophysites led him to promote a theological orientation where Chalcedon was not any longer to be considered and understood in itself, but only in the light of Alexandrian Christology. The Council of 553, a result of his efforts, can therefore be considered a real ecumenical event in the modern sense of the word "ecumenical." It developed a reformulation of dogma for no other sake than that of the "separated brethren."

The problem of "historical relativism" in its relation to the very content of the Christian message is therefore inseparable from the notions of the "old" and the "new," Adam and Christ, flesh and Spirit. The historical Church, the Church *in via*, unavoidably uses the categories of the world: philosophy, authority, law. These categories belong to the "fallen" and yet unredeemed world. However, what makes the Church to be the *Church of God* is that she is not determined in her very being by these categories, and her existence has meaning only if redemption is at work in her midst. Her mission consists in making men see *beyond* these categories of the fallen world and to live in God, in freedom, in at least a partial experience of absolute Truth.

*Formgeschichte* makes us see the biblical authors as living, historical individuals in their human settings, and familiarizes us with the categories of their minds. It thus helps immensely our understanding of Scripture. However, it totally defeats its purpose when it imposes on us as ultimate the categories of scientific research or of modern existential philosophy, or reduces itself to linguistic analysis, or considers as myth anything which is not physically or historically demonstrable. It then destroys the very content of the biblical message: liberation of man from cosmic determinism, which is witnessed by the empty tomb and the Resurrection.

The use of philosophical, scientific, or legal categories by the Church is a dynamic process. The goal is man's transfiguration, his entrance into the Kingdom. He is not to remain a prisoner of rational or cosmic limitations. Greek philosophy, which was once adopted as the *milieu* of Christian theology because its categories were then the only understandable ones, was never absolutized as such. Did Aristotelian terms like *hypostasis* and *physis* keep their full original meaning in the Chalcedonian definition? Would Aristotle himself understand Basil of Caesarea? The new Christian meaning of these terms remained basically unacceptable for those in the ancient world who rejected the historical Christ of the New Testament. The dynamic, free, and critical attitude toward Greek philosophy which characterized the patristic period, and which implied an often painful process of discrimination as well as many individual mistakes, can be studied with great profit in our challenging days of change. Perhaps a greater parallelism than first appears can be drawn even between Origen and Rudolf Bultmann. The former was an honest Christian and founder of biblical scholarship, who surrendered Christianity to the Neoplatonic world view which was his own and that of his contemporaries. The latter was an honest Christian demythologizing the New Testament and thus trying to meet the consensus of modern existentialism.

## Conclusions

I am fully conscious of the fact that this paper does not sufficiently analyze the problem of "historical relativism" from the philosophic or systematic points of view. Its purpose is mainly to examine the problem of authority as seen through history and patristic theology.

There can be little doubt that the development of church "authority" which took place in the West during the Middle Ages and continued in Post-Tridentine Roman Catholicism has been determined by the concern to protect the existence in history of a God-established absolute reality, the Church. The inevitable presupposition of all those who contributed to this development, from the canonists of the Gregorian Reform to the Fathers of the First Vatican Council, was that the continuity and strength of the Church could be *guaranteed* only through infallible authority. This concern was enhanced by the prevalent Augustinian concept of man as intrinsically sinful and liable to errors. The establishment by God of an infallible authority was thus an act of divine charity for man, to preserve him from himself and his own errors.

The various Western reactions against this structure are well-known: the conciliar movement with its substitution of a standing committee of bishops for the papacy, the Reformation in its various forms ranging from biblical fundamentalism to pentecostal individualism, and finally, today, secularism, Christian or not. It is interesting to note

that A. S. Khomiakov sees in this entire Western development a common "scepticism." It is to meet *doubt* that the
security of an external authority—the Pope, or the Bible—
is necessary;[13] and consequently, doubt triumphs where
authority is absent.

The recent decisions of Vatican II have certainly contributed greatly to creating the state of flux in which the
Christian world finds itself today. The entire movement to
enhance Roman authority, which was in constant progress
since the early Middle Ages until the pontificate of Pius XII
inclusively, has been reversed by John XXIII and his council. It is not yet clear, however, how far and in what direction the Roman Catholic Church will be able to move without disavowing the very principle upon which its previous
development was based, for it is clear that this principle remains intact in the constitution *De ecclesia*. The Roman
Pontiff remains the ultimate and "external" criterion of the
Church's unity and infallibility. The episcopal college depends on him, but he does not ultimately depend upon the
college, and thus remains the final "security."

If Orthodox theology has any contribution to make to
the present ecumenical dialogue, it will consist in stressing
and showing the *auxiliary* character of authority. It is not
authority which makes the Church to be the Church, but the
Spirit alone, acting in the Church as Body, realizing the sacramental presence of Christ Himself among men and in men.
Authority in the bishops, the councils, Scripture, and Tradition only expresses this presence, but does not replace the
goal of human life in Christ. That goal is to experience and
live the Kingdom of God which has already appeared but is
also still expected to come as the ultimate end of all things.

Such a view is not emotionalism or subjectivism or mysticism, because the locus of the personal experience is the
communion of the saints, constituting the Church, and implying openness, love, and self-denial in the framework of
a sacramental-hierarchical structure. It is not mere intellectual knowledge. To the question, "How do I know?" there
is no other Christian answer than, "Come and see!"

[13]*Op. cit.*, p. 54.

# 3

# What Is an Ecumenical Council? *

The Second Vatican Council provoked a great resurgence of ecclesiological thought in Western Christendom. Innumerable publications, both scholarly and popular, appeared in many countries about the conciliar institution, its origin, its history, and its contemporary significance. This interest for ecclesiology, and particularly for the theme of "conciliarity" has since subsided. It was succeeded by a trend which discarded all forms of "institutionalism"; ecclesiology has ceased to be a popular subject. "Secular" interpretations of Christianity and, more recently, various forms of "charismaticism" have made "ecclesiology" as such seemingly unnecessary. The Church has in some quarters come to be considered as an idol and an obstacle either to man's acceptance of his real responsibility in history, or to his immediate experience of the spiritual gifts.

It seems to me that we are presently on the eve of a return to the traditional theme of the Church as "Mystery" and as Temple of the Spirit. For if the inadequacy of "secular Christianity" has been rather generally understood (especially by that part of the younger generation which searches for a religion of experience), the insufficiencies and the dangers of an extra-ecclesial charismaticism have become equally evident. "The Church is the *locus* of the Spirit's action, and in the Church the Spirit is the principle of life

*Paper delivered at the *Stiftungfonds Pro Oriente*, Vienna, Austria, on May 5, 1972, and originally published in *St. Vladimir's Theological Quarterly* vol. 17:4 (1973), pp. 259-73.

and action."[1] This pneumatological approach to the Church, as recently expressed by an Orthodox theologian, has been much too often forgotten, or too narrowly restricted to the notions of power or institutional authority. Sound ecclesiology alone can reconcile experience and responsibility, continuity and change, authority and freedom. And this reconciliation is a continuous process, effected by the Spirit.

The object of this paper is to attempt a definition of the ecclesiological notions which stood behind the conciliar institution of the past, so that the present and the future may be seen in the light of "the same Spirit" (cf. I Cor. 12:11). For a council is primarily a *church event*, and only as such can it possess significance and validity. A council's function and mission can be understood only in an ecclesiological framework.

## I. The Foundations of Conciliarity

The first "councils" of the Church were not organized by anyone. No scriptural or ecclesiastical authority ever "instituted" them or gave them procedural directions. Obviously the early councils grew out of the very *nature* of the Christian faith as it was understood by the early Christians. It is clear, for example, that the result of Christ's ministry and the apostles' witness to that ministry resulted in the establishment of a messianic *community* which received the Spirit at Pentecost. This community understood and proclaimed the meaning of the Christ-event, and formed the group from which the various New Testament writings took stage, described in the first twelve chapters of the Book of the faith" through a series of doctrinal crises and debates.

In the life of this community there was a first initial stage, described in the first twelve chapters of the Book of Acts. The community was coextensive with the church of Jerusalem and was led by the "Twelve," headed by Peter. It was an eschatological community, witnessing to the realiza-

---

[1]N. Afanas'ev, *Tserkov Dukha Sviatogo* ("The Church of the Holy Spirit," Paris, 1971), p. 283.

tion *in Sion* of the messianic prophecies. Conciliarity, which included "the multitude of the disciples" (Acts 6:2) convoked by the "Twelve," was practiced whenever important decisions such as the election of the "seven" were to be taken. The pattern of corporate decisions in *each* local church was a form of conciliarity which remained constant in early Christianity. Later it expressed itself in the election of bishops "by all the people" (Hippolytus, *Apost. Tr.* I, 2) and in the Cyprianic principle: *episcopus in ecclesia and ecclesia in episcopo.*

The moment when this pattern, which was that of the mother-church of Jerusalem, was adopted by Christian communities *outside* of Jerusalem was a crucial step in the history of early Christianity. As the Gospel began to spread in the Gentile world through the ministry of Paul, new communities were founded throughout the entire Roman world. Each of these communities was to be the *same* Church. In each one the same eucharistic meal was celebrated, transforming the community into the Body of Christ. In the writings of the Apostolic Fathers, especially St. Ignatius of Antioch, each of these local churches was seen as *the catholic church*, i.e. each time that "two of three were gathered" in the name of Christ, He was present with them fully. The gathering was not a "part" of the Body, but the Body itself, *caput et corpus.*

The passage from the original state of affairs when "the Church" was the church in Jerusalem only, to the new situation when "the Church" was to be the *same* Church also in Antioch, in Corinth, and in Rome, is described in the account of the "apostolic council" in Jerusalem (Acts 15). Not only did this assembly make a momentous decision, recognizing the universal character of the Christian Gospel, but silently it also acknowledged a radical change in the structure and, therefore, the significance of the Jerusalemite church itself. Since Peter had gone "to another place" (Acts 12:17), the leadership of the mother-church went to James. At the assembly itself the "Twelve" are not mentioned, but the leadership belongs to "the apostles and presbyters" (Acts 15:6).

This leadership is later defined even more specifically as that of "James and the presbyters" (Acts 21:18).[2]

These details are important for our purpose, because they illustrate well two different ecclesiological situations. The gathering, or "council," of the "Twelve" in Jerusalem was the supreme witness to the truth of Christ's resurrection, a joint proclamation of the Gospel by the eye-witnesses themselves. Later, however, the eye-witnesses were dispersed, and the "apostolic" faith which they had proclaimed needed to be maintained by the "churches." There was, therefore, a need to preserve the *consensus*, the unity, the coherence between the churches. This task was fulfilled by the councils.

The prevailing ecclesiology of the sub-apostolic Church, as found in Ignatius and in Irenaeus, is a "eucharistic" ecclesiology. The Church was truly the "Church of God," wherever it was found, because it witnessed every Sunday the presence of Christ in the mystery of the common meal. Only such an ecclesiology could allow Ignatius to say, "Where Christ Jesus is, there is the Catholic Church" (*Smyrn.* 8:2). It is also that ecclesiology alone which can explain the fact that the so-called "monarchical episcopate" (one "bishop" in each eucharistic community or "church") was to be universally accepted without any significant controversy. There would have been ample room for collective or collegial leadership in each church if there had been no internal necessity for someone to "take the place of God by presiding over the community" (Ignatius, *Magn.* 6:1; cf. *Trall.* 2, 3:1-2). In fact, the presbyterium did assume the role of a directing in all fields of church life, *other than* the sacramental.

The Eucharist required a "president," someone sitting at the very place of Christ. From Acts one can easily infer that

[2]The importance of Acts 12:17 for the understanding of the ministry of Peter is well defined by Oscar Cullmann in *Peter: Disciple, Apostle, Martyr* (Philadelphia, 1962); on the consequences for the understanding of early Christian ecclesiology, see my book, *Orthodoxy and Catholicity* (New York: Sheed and Ward, 1966), pp. 8-10; cf. also J. Zizioulas, "The Development of Conciliar Structures to the Time of the First Ecumenical Council," in *Councils and the Ecumenical Movement* (World Council of Churches Studies 5, Geneva, 1968), pp. 36-37.

Peter fulfilled that role in the original community in Jerusalem, where he was later succeeded by James. In all other churches, however, "bishops" were elected locally and then invested with the "apostolic" function of preserving the original faith. *Everywhere* the Eucharist was the same Eucharist because there was only one Christ, one Church, one "apostolic" faith, and one and the same Spirit, guiding the Church in "all Truth."

St. Peter had received from the Lord Himself the solemn promise: "You are Peter and on this rock I will build my Church" (Matt. 16:18), and this *logion* of Jesus was preserved, in St. Matthew, the Gospel of the church of Jerusalem, where Peter presided over the Eucharist and was the spokesman of the Church against which "the powers of hell shall not prevail." But the Church—the same Church—was to be established elsewhere and others inherited also the promise given to Peter.

As early as St. Ignatius the image of the episcopate is associated with the image of the "rock" (*To Polycarp* 1:1). With Cyprian of Carthage the idea that each bishop, as the head and pastor of his local church, was a successor of St. Peter and the "rock" of faith was expressed quite clearly. Most scholars agree that for Cyprian the succession of Peter is in no way limited to Rome. Every local church is "the Church," and as such inherits the promise given to Peter. "God is one," he writes, "and Christ is one, and one is the Church, and there is one chair, founded on Peter by the Lord's command." (*Deus unus est et Christus unus et una ecclesia et cathedra una super Petrum Domini voce fundata, Ep.* 43:5.) This understanding follows necessarily from a "eucharistic" conception of the Church. If each local church is the Church *in its fullness*, the "catholic Church," it must indeed be identical with that Church which was mentioned by Jesus Himself in Matt. 16:18, the Church founded on Peter.

Careful reading in the patristic Tradition, both Greek and Latin, indicates that this understanding was by no means limited to Cyprian, but prevailed in the minds of the major theologians. There was no formal elaboration of the idea, however, because "ecclesiology" was never treated systematically. St. Gregory of Nyssa speaks of the power of the keys transmitted by Peter to the bishops (*De castigatione*, P.G. 46:312 C), and even Pseudo-Dionysius sees in Peter the prototype of the order of the "high priests" (*Eccl. Hier.* 7, 7). In the later period, especially after 1204 when a Latin patriarch was confirmed as bishop of Constantinople by the pope, Byzantine theologians began to use the argument against Rome: the pope is not the *only* successor of Peter, but all the bishops share equally in that dignity.[3]

The concept of the "local church," headed by a bishop normally elected by his church, but also assuming a charismatic and apostolic function as "successor of Peter," is the doctrinal basis of conciliarity as it began to be regularly practiced beginning in the third century. For "eucharistic ecclesiology" is not congregationalism. It presupposes that each local church, while it possesses the fullness of catholicity, is always in unity and fellowship with all the other churches sharing the same catholicity. The bishops are not only morally responsible for this fellowship, but also they *are* sharing in a single episcopal ministry. On this point Cyprian again has coined the decisive phrase, "The episcopate is one, of which each bishop holds his part in its totality." (*Episcopatus unus est, cuius a singulis in solidum pars tenetur, De Cath. Eccl. unitate*, 5.) Each bishop exercises his ministry *with* the other bishops because his ministry is identical to that of the others and the Church is one.

The most ancient tradition of the Church requires conciliarity at the moment of the episcopal consecration, which is accomplished in the presence and with the participation of several bishops (cf. Hippolytus, *Apost. Tr.* 1). Similarly, the agreement of several bishops on a controversial issue of doctrine or discipline was considered as a more convincing *sign* of the "faith of Peter" than the testimony of a single bishop. Irenaeus had already discovered that the *tradition* of the apostles, transmitted without interruption by the succession of bishops, was a decisive criterion of truth. To this consensus "in time" he had also added a consensus "in

[3]See J. Meyendorff *et al., The Primacy of Peter in the Orthodox Church* (London: Faith Press, 1963), pp. 14-29.

space": the *same* tradition was confessed by all the bishops "everywhere in every church" (*traditionem apostolorum in toto mundo manifestatam in omni ecclesia, Adversus haereses, III, 3, 1*). The most logical and immediate way of checking such a consensus, at least partially, was the provincial council.

The African Church in the third century left us with a great amount of information concerning the councils, and the ecclesiological presuppositions of the conciliar institution there were those of the Catholic Church everywhere. We know of councils being held in Asia Minor, in Antioch, and elsewhere. In 325 the Council of Nicaea generalized the practice in the framework of the new imperial system which it endorsed. A council of bishops in each province was to meet twice a year to discuss all pending ecclesiastical questions and to act as court to solve conflicts (canons 4 and 5 of Nicaea).

Once "institutionalized" this regular episcopal conciliarity ran the danger of obliterating the very principle of ecclesiology on which it was based. Indeed, on the one hand, it tended to supersede the the original "local" conciliarity, which comprised each bishop, his presbyterium, and his people. This was inevitable since the provincial council tended to act as an authority *over* the local churches and *over* individual bishops. On the other hand, the provincial councils began to use the *legal* procedures of Roman courts, accepting for example the principle of majority vote (canon 6 of Nicaea). This evolution, which started even before Constantine, was perhaps inevitable and practically useful; but it created an internal tension between the basic ecclesiological ideal of a *consensus*, based upon the *charisma veritatis* of *each* bishop (cf. Irenaeus, *Adversus haereses*, IV, 16, 2), and the legal and practical requirements of a formal assembly, patterned after the rules of secular society and invested with legal power. It should be noted, however, that the influence of secular legalism upon conciliar procedures concerned mostly the issues of church order and discipline. The solution of *credal* matters continued generally to be sought as a charismatic consensus, with each bishop giving his own testimonium. Total unity in faith and in eucharistic com-

munion were required as a *condition* for an authoritative
statement to be made by the council, and for the council itself to be considered an authentic council of the *Church*.
"The *koinonia* of the eucharistic gathering constituted the
ground on which conciliarity found its 'raison d'être.' "[4]


## II. Ecumenical Councils

Whatever judgement contemporary historians pass on the
emperor Constantine, it clearly appears from the numerous
documents available that he did his best to exercise his newly
assumed role of protector of the Church in a way which
would be in conformity with the traditions of the Church
itself. He did not want to create a new church. Hence he
continually urged the Church to use its own authority to
solve the issues of the day. He knew of the authority of the
councils, but understood them pragmatically as assemblies
of ecclesiastical officials competent in their own field and,
therefore, qualified to take authoritative stands. The charismatic nature of the councils could not be of any use to the
Roman State (or to any state for that matter). The State
was asking unity and order from the councils. However, the
latter did not consider unity and order as ends in themselves,
but as values lower than faithfulness to apostolic Tradition
and Truth. In order to solve the Donatist controversy in
Africa Constantine thought it proper to use the conciliar institution in an attempt to conciliate the estranged group. "I
have decided," he writes to pope Miltiades, "that Caecilian
himself, with ten of the bishops who apparently are accusing
him, and ten others regarded by him as essential to his case,
shall sail for Rome. He will be granted a hearing in such
conditions as you will judge proper under the most sacred
law ... Such is the regard I pay to the lawful Catholic Church
that I desire you to leave no schism or division of any kind
anywhere." (Eusebius, *Eccl. Hist.* X, 5, 15-22.)

No Roman Emperor has ever been so respectful of a

[4]J. Zizioulas, *op. cit.*, p. 41.

religious group and its traditions, but also so obviously mis-
led concerning his ability to deal with it. His attempts, and
those of his successors, to force the Church to express itself
in terms of the *pax Romana*—law, order, unity—never succeeded. The Roman State wanted the councils to function
and to issue decisions with the legal clarity and regularity of
the Roman courts, but this goal was never attained.

In spite of his failure to settle the Donatist crisis, Constantine, advised by Osius of Cordoba, embarked on an
even more generous enterprise, the convocation of an "ecumenical" council in Nicaea. The idea was in full conformity
with the developing concepts of conciliarity. A consensus
reached between *all* the bishops of the world would indeed
be the highest possible witness to the "unity of the episcopate" preached by St. Cyprian and, therefore, the most
authoritative way of proclaiming the true Christian doctrine.
However, the two irreconcilable logics of the State and of
the Church shaped the history of the successive "ecumenical"
councils. For the Empire, an ecumenical council was convoked by the emperor in order to provide him with a statement which was to become imperial law. For the Church,
a council was nothing more than a "witness" to the Truth, a
witness which could prove in fact to be a false one. Whatever the inroads of the Hellenistic idea of the "emperor-
god" in the consciousness of Christians, there was never
among them "any moral or theological obligation to believe
that the emperor had the power to define Christian dogma."[5]
Neither imperial convocation nor imperial confirmation were
considered automatic guarantees of infallibility.

The history of the Nicene definition, which Constantine himself eventually rejected and which did not receive
universal acceptance until 381, is instructive. The history of
the "reception" or "rejection" of other councils is well-known
to historians but remains an embarrassment to those theologians who seek clear-cut external criteria of the Church's infallibility.

There are three negative points illustrating the history of

[5]See J. Meyendorff, "Justinian, the Empire and the Church," in *Dumbarton Oaks Papers* vol. 22 (1968), pp. 50-51.

the councils which are of great importance for our own times. (1) The word "ecumenical," in the sense in which it was used by early Christians and throughout the Middle Ages, has meaning only in the context of the Byzantine "symphony" between Church and Empire. It cannot be translated simply as "imperial" because the Empire recognized in matters of faith the competence of the bishops and the power of public opinion. The interminable doctrinal controversies over the Trinity and the person of Christ prove the fact that the emperor was powerless in imposing theological statements by decree, and that the "ecumenical" councils convoked by him never enjoyed automatic infallibility. Byzantine society never accepted the idea that the mystery of the Church could be reduced to the legal principles of the *pax Romana*. A clear and short definition of an ecumenical council is given by the Byzantine historian Cedrenus (eleventh cent.): Councils "were named ecumenical, because bishops of the whole Roman Empire were invited by imperial orders and in each of them, and especially in these six councils, there was discussion of the faith and a vote, i.e. dogmatic formulae were promulgated." (*Hist.* I, 3, ed. Bonn, 1838, p. 39.) Since the Byzantine emperor was considered as the protector of all Christians, the "ecumenical" councils held doctrinal validity even beyond the border of the empire. However, even inside the empire their acceptance was not automatic. "Ecumenical" councils were convoked in Sardica (343), Rimini (359), Ephesus (449), Constantinople (754), etc., which were eventually either rejected, or accepted only as "local councils." A gap always remained between the ecclesiological significance of a universal episcopal consensus, which "ecumenical" councils were supposed to represent, and the political management of church affairs in the framework of the Roman *oikoumene*. The word "ecumenical" itself reflects the Byzantine politico-religious view of society. The patriarch of Constantinople was called "ecumenical" because of his responsibility in the empire, and the head of the imperial university merited the title *oikoumenikos didaskalos.*[6]

[6]See the excellent review of the problem in J. Anastasiou, "What is the Meaning of the Word 'ecumenical' in Relation to the Councils?" in *Councils*

It is, therefore, obviously impossible to transpose the Byzantine criteria of "ecumenicity" to our own times. With the disappearance of the Empire these criteria have necessarily disappeared also. Only the concept of an episcopal consensus, which the "ecumenical councils" reflected when they were recognized by the Church, remains fully valid.

(2) The second negative point concerning the history of the ecumenical councils is related to the problem of their degree of representation. No council of the past ever included *all* the bishops of the Church, or even approached the representative character of our world assemblies which enjoy the facilities of modern communication systems. In 430, for example, imperial invitations were sent to the provincial metropolitans of the Eastern Empire and to a rather arbitrary selection of Western bishops (cf. Mansi, *Collectio amplissima* ... 4, cols. 1112-1116). It was understood that the representatives of the Roman pope were to be present. However, at the Council of 381 the West was not represented at all, and in 553 Justinian went ahead with the Fifth Council in spite of Pope Vigilius' refusal to participate. Legal "ecumenicity" was formally conditioned by the imperial convocation and approval only. Ecclesiologically, however, the authority of a council depended upon its being the true voice of the episcopal and ecclesial consensus. Hence the importance of the approval by Rome, whose "priority" in church affairs was recognized. Approval by the West was also desirable from the point of view of Byzantine imperial universalism, as the West was theoretically a part of the Empire.

(3) The third point concerns the relation between an "ecumenical" council and church unity. It is quite clear, at least in the first millenium, that an "ecumenical" council was not conceived as a "union council" between separated churches. It presupposed doctrinal unity and eucharistic communion between the participants. There is, therefore, a clear difference between the prevailing use of the word "ecumenical" today and the meaning it had when it was applied to the early councils. In this respect it is easy to recall the

*and the Ecumenical Movement* (World Council of Churches Studies 5, Geneva, 1968), pp. 27-31.

attitude of St. Cyril of Alexandria towards Nestorius in 431, that of Dioscorus towards Flavian in 449, and that of the Roman legates at Chalcedon towards Dioscorus in 451. In each of these cases doctrinal difference required the "Orthodox" bishops to sit as council, and the suspected heretics to occupy seats "in the middle," i.e. as defendants. Also, at the great Photian council of 879-880 the recognition and solemn proclamation of Photius as legitimate patriarch and "concelebrant" by Pope John VIII necessarily preceded their council together.[7]

The idea of a "union council," i.e. a council between the churches of East and West after the schism, was promoted by the Greek side in the late Middle Ages in an effort to restore union. The papacy was reluctant to accept the concept. It obtained a Roman confession of faith from Emperor Michael VIII Palaeologus *before* the union of Lyons (1274). However, many Greeks in the fourteenth century attributed the failure of union attempts precisely to the fact that no true conciliar procedure was followed. Several offers of a union council were thus made on behalf of the Byzantines. These included not only the project presented to Pope Benedict XII in 1339 by Barlaam of Calabria,[8] but also several offers made by the conservative monastic leadership which took over the Byzantine Church after 1347. In 1367 the emperor-monk John Cantacuzenos, speaking to the papal legate Paul on behalf of the Greek Church, offered "to hold a catholic and ecumenical council," with provision that "the bishops who are under the ecumenical patriarch, those close-by and those far-off, that is the metropolitans of Russia with some of his bishops, of Trebizond, of Alania, of Zechia, may gather together in Constantinople, as well as the other patriarchs, those of Alexandria, of Antioch and of Jerusalem, and also the catholicos of Iberia (Georgia), the patriarch of Trnovo and the archbishop of Serbia, and that

[7]See F. Dvornik, *The Photian Schism: History and Legend* (Cambridge, 1948), pp. 184-185.

[8]See C. Gianelli, "Un progetto di Barlaam per l'unione delle Chiese," in *Miscellanea G. Mercati* vol. 3 (*Studi e testi* vol. 123, Città del Vaticano, 1946), pp. 185-201.

representatives of the pope may come."[9] The project was officially approved by the Synod and the patriarchs of Alexandria and Jerusalem; the hesychast patriarch Philotheos Kokkinos announced the news to the archbishop of Ochrid and informed him that "agreement was reached with the pope's envoys that, if our doctrine (i.e. that of the Eastern Church) will be shown at the council to be superior to that of the Latins, they will join us and confess it" (Miklosich-Müller, *Acta*, I, 492).

Rejected by Pope Urban V in 1369, the project was to be revived after the triumph of "conciliarist" theories in the West, and would finally result in the council of Ferrara-Florence. The monastic-conservative party in Byzantium, led by Mark of Ephesus, remained faithful to its acceptance of the idea of a union council. Obviously the title of "ecumenical" was applied to it from the very beginning, for it indeed reflected the Byzantine idea of the *oikoumene*, East and West.

Was the concept of a "union council," i.e. a council held without the possibility for all its members to have eucharistic communion with each other, justified ecclesiologically? This is, indeed, a question which contemporary ecumenical thought must answer. The failure of Florence greatly weakens the point of those who would promote a similar approach today. In any case, the problem is essentially ecclesiological. To be a *true* council, a council must be a council of the *Church*. But can there be a Church outside of eucharistic unity? And can there be eucharistic unity without a single united commitment to the one true apostolic faith? The dilemma remains intact, and the idea of an "ecumenical" council as such can hardly help in finding a solution.

Whatever its involvement with the imperial ideal of "ecumenicity" and its insistence on the role of "ecumenical" councils as supreme witnesses of the Christian truth, the Byzantine Church never thought that such councils were the

[9]See J. Meyendorff, "Projects de concile oecuménique en 1367: un dialogue inédit entre Jean Cantacuzène et le légat Paul," in *Dumbarton Oaks Papers* vol. 14 (1960), p. 173.

*only* source of the Church's magisterium or the only criterion of the Holy Spirit's action in the Church. As centuries of separation with the West went by, the idea of "ecumenicity" gradually acquired a more secular and political meaning. An "ecumenical" council was seen as a council with the West, restoring the old Roman *oikoumene*, a sort of "ecumenical conference" in our own modern sense. But this was not needed for the preservation of true Orthodox Christianity, which was fully expressed through the teaching of the bishops, the liturgy, and the Eastern councils, which did not (and could not) claim a political "ecumenicity" but were still seen as true witnesses of the Tradition. The numerous doctrinal statements made by local synods were included in the *Synodikon* of the First Sunday of Lent ("Sunday of Orthodoxy") and thus became integrated in the liturgical experience of the Church. These comprised several decisions of twelfth-century councils, but most important were the statements of the Palamite councils of the fourteenth century. Never were these statements considered as either temporary or incomplete simply because they were not proclaimed by an "ecumenical" council.

### III. Councils today

Now that we are clearly out of both the "Byzantine" and the "post-Byzantine" periods of church history, the problem of realizing "conciliarity" is a burning issue for the Orthodox Church and for the whole of Christendom. Clearly enough, it is rather in the experience of the early Church than in later Byzantine and medieval developments that one can discover the *permanent* ecclesiological elements which make the Church to be the same "apostolic" Church always. Of course, the experience of the Middle Ages cannot be rejected altogether, and the situation of the pre-Constantinian age cannot simply be reproduced today, but the permanent *identity* of the Church needs to be articulated, as it transcends the passing and changing historical conditions of the past or of the present.

In an attempt to illustrate the problem concretely I will discuss briefly three practical and interrelated issues which challenge the contemporary Orthodox thought about conciliarity.

(1)   A Pan-Orthodox Council is presently in the stage of preparation. I want to avoid here the political issues (which may actually decide whether the council will be held or not) and concentrate on ecclesiology proper.

In the light of church history, contemporary Orthodox thought must liberate itself from the idea that a council, whether "ecumenical" or not, possesses a legally automatic infallibility. So much has been said and written about the Orthodox Church being a "conciliar" church, about the "seven ecumenical councils" as the only criteria of Orthodoxy, that many contemporary Orthodox churchmen are literally afraid of the idea of a council because they know their own inability to act "infallibly." Conciliar activity requires courage and presupposes a "risk of faith." True councils have always been spiritual *events*, when the Spirit of God was able to transcend the human limitations of the members so that the council became the voice of God Himself. Such an event requires a spiritual and theological readiness, which may or may not be a reality today.

Fortunately, the Church's "conciliarity" can express itself by means other than through formal councils. Whatever can be said of its limitations and of the Hegelian roots of some of its expressions, the thought of the nineteenth-century Russian lay theologian A. S. Khomiakov has given to the Orthodox world a new consciousness of the fact that Truth in the Church does not depend upon any infallible institution, but is an experience always available in the *communion* of the Church. Of course this communion is understood both as faithfulness to Tradition and as openness to the *consensus fidelium* today.

But the theory of *sobornost'* as expressed by Khomiakov and his disciples has also raised new problems. In reference to the conciliar institution itself it led a majority of Russian theologians to affirm that councils require the active, direct, and responsible participation of the laity. The question then arises of the particular functions of the episcopate. Since 1917, in the Russian Church laymen have been admitted as full voting members of the provincial councils, while the bishops keep a collective veto-power. There is no doubt that the Council of Moscow (1917-1918) held under those conditions was a significant and authentic expression of conciliarity in the midst of revolutionary changes, and that it contributed much to the survival of the Church in the following tragic decades. But are the principles of democratic "representation" of the episcopate, the clergy, and the laity, as distinct "classes" of Christians, truly adequate from the ecclesiological point of view? Did not the early Christian church structure of small dioceses, *local* eucharistic conciliarity of the bishop and the presbyterium, and full lay responsibility in the life of the local eucharistic community—lead to provincial and "ecumenical" councils of bishops alone? However, since "local conciliarity" does not exist, is not *sobornost'* at the higher level, provincial or ecumenical, a valid (possibly temporary) substitute?

These questions remain unanswered in contemporary Orthodox theology, and the membership of a future Pan-Orthodox Council does not seem to be clearly defined.

(2) The second area where the authority and significance of "ecumenical" councils is obviously at stake is to be found in the conversations with Non-Chalcedonian Eastern Churches. Clearly the tradition with which they are presently identified is under the formal condemnation of councils which the Orthodox Church accepts as "ecumenical." On the other hand recent historical research and theological dialogue seem to indicate that agreement on the *substance* of the christology which appeared as the reason for the original schism can easily be reached. Another irony of the situation is that the Non-Chalcedonian Churches confess and practice an ecclesiology which is identical to that of the Orthodox Church. They too recognize the authority of "ecumenical" councils, but they refuse to "receive" Chalcedon (an attitude which is parallel to that adopted by the Byzantine Orthodox towards, for example, the councils of Rimini and Florence, with the exception that the Orthodox today reject also the

doctrine approved at Rimini and at Florence, while the Non-Chalcedonians seem to agree that the substance if not the language of Chalcedon is Orthodox). The way towards an understanding would therefore seem to pass through a bilateral adoption of a *formula concordiae* similar to that of 433, and in the spirit of the attitude of the Fifth Council (533), which canonized the christology of St. Cyril while affirming the Chalcedonian faith as well. This approach raises the problems of *continuity* and *consistency* of Tradition, which are far from being solved yet. It also questions the relation between the verbal expression of a doctrine and its true content and asks which of the two is really covered by the authority of councils.

(3) The third question which is brought by some before contemporary Orthodox consciousness is whether it is possible to hold an "ecumenical" council in the present state of division of the Christian world. It seems to me that such a question is as misleading as the meaning of the word "ecumenical." On the one hand, it is clear that there was *never* a time when the Christian world was truly united. All the "ecumenical" councils of the past have in fact been divisive, and some among the most important (like Chalcedon) have remained divisive to this very day. One should also remember that the ministry of Jesus Himself and His teaching brought about schism between Israel and the Church, and was indeed a "division" (Luke 12:51). Not simply "unity," but *unity in Christ* is the very basis of any "conciliar" act. It is precisely on this point that the Roman imperial idea of "ecumenicity," which sought a socio-political unification of the world using religion as a tool, could never coincide with Christian universalism. The latter may have used the facilities and the ideology of the empire to pursue its own goals, but it could never be identified with it.

One of the most basic premises of Orthodox ecclesiology is that the unity of the Church is not man-made, but is a gift of God which can only be *received* and (if lost) rediscovered. It does not depend, therefore, on either a Byzantino-Roman, or a modern "Pan-Christian" universalism. The Orthodox Church may indeed avoid using the word "ecumen-

ical" to designate its councils because of the past and present
ambiguities attached to that word, but it cannot admit (without renouncing its entire Tradition) that authoritative and
"true" Christian teaching, normally expressed in councils,
has become impossible after either the fifth- or the eleventh-
century schisms. The Church of Christ could not have ceased
to exist or to share in the presence of the Spirit, "teaching
all things" (John 14:25).


### Conclusion

Churches, as human *institutions*, and also the various organized forms of the ecumenical movement, are naturally
driven to seek *institutional* formulae which would help bring
about unity among divided Christians in a way which would
be consistent with their respective pasts. However, if that
unity is to be the one that God wills, there are no shortcuts
to it which could avoid ecclesiology. Institutions exist to reflect and protect the nature of the Church, not to modify it.
This certainly applies also to the idea of an "ecumenical"
council. Whatever adjective one uses to designate an assembly gathered in the name of Christ, its ultimate authenticity depends upon the presence of the Spirit, which has
been promised to the *Church*. History helps us in discerning
the variety of ways through which the Spirit has spoken—
through "ecumenical" councils and outside of them. It shows
as well the diverse and tortuous tissue of human failures and
mistakes. The greatest and actually the *only* Christian hope
lies in the fact that God is stronger than human history. Let
us not place our hope elsewhere and miss the Spirit of God,
who is never imprisoned in history, but like the wind "blows
where it wills" (John 3:8). To quote St. Irenaeus, "Where
the Church is, there is the Spirit of God; and where the Spirit
of God is, there is the Church and every kind of grace, and
the Spirit is truth" (*Adversus haereses* III, 24, 1).

# 4

# Rome and Orthodoxy: Is "Authority" Still the Issue?*

The place of the Orthodox Church in the ecumenical dialogue which developed in this century has always been peculiar. This was inevitable because the basic concerns and the main presuppositions of the movement were shaped by the historical features of Western Christianity, Roman Catholic and Protestant. However, the situation is now in the process of changing because the concepts of "East" and "West," while keeping their significance in terms of theological tradition, have lost much of their geographical and cultural meaning. Though a small minority, the Orthodox Church is now actively present in traditionally Western countries, particularly the United States. On the other hand, areas like Greece, the Balkans, and Russia, where Orthodox Christianity has been predominant also belong to the "West," if one compares them to the newly emerging societies of Asia and Africa.

In this new situation, the ecclesiological issue which has traditionally separated Rome and Orthodoxy cannot be envisaged simply as a cultural phenomenon which would consequently be bound to disappear as an issue. Even if one holds this "cultural" and purely "historical" interpretation of the schism, denying that any real theological and ecclesiological

*Revised version of a paper delivered at the *Stiftungfonds Pro Oriente*, Vienna, Austria, in 1975, and originally published in French in the periodical *Istina* vol. 20 (1975); a slightly different version appeared in *A Pope For All Christians?*, ed. Peter J. McCord (New York: Paulist Press, 1976).

issues separate the churches today, one is obligated to produce a theologically sound and ecclesiologically workable model of a "united church." Unavoidably the traditional issue of *authority* again emerges as the central question; and one discovers that it cannot be solved without recourse to Scripture and Tradition, for without the latter Christianity ceases to be Christ's and the Church is not the Church "of God."

In recent years relations between the Orthodox Church and Rome have gone through a series of quite extraordinary events, which certainly would not have been predictable in the preceding generation. These include an exchange of documents, "lifting the anathemas" of 1054, and several personal meetings between the pope and the patriarch of Constantinople. All of these events directly involved the question of authority, and particularly *papal* authority; but none of them provided an articulate and definitive *solution* to the issue. The events were largely *symbolic* in nature: speeches, gestures, and actions which changed the atmosphere. It is the task of theologians today to discover how these events can be interpreted and used, not for the narrow sake of ecclesiastical diplomacy, or even of "Orthodox-Catholic relations" (only one aspect of our responsibility for a united Christian witness), but for the true solution of the problem of authority in the Church, without which no real Christian unity is possible.

In any case, since in this question of authority the Orthodox tradition is strikingly distinct from Western Christendom as a whole,[1] an Orthodox contribution to the present stage of the debate is crucially important.


## I. The schism: two ecclesiologies

One of the most striking facts about the schism between the East and the West is that it cannot be *dated*. In the common declaration published in December 7, 1965, by Pope Paul and Patriarch Athenagoras, the events of 1054 are re-

---

[1]On this particular issue see my book *Orthodoxy and Catholicity* (New York: Sheed and Ward, 1966), pp. 119-140, and also Chapter 2, above.

duced to their real and actually rather insignificant proportions. "Among the obstacles which exist on the way towards the development of brotherly relations of confidence and esteem (between the churches), we find the remembrance of the decisions, acts, and painful incidents which led in 1054 to the sentence of excommunication published against Patriarch Michael Cerularius and two other persons by the legates of the Roman see, headed by Cardinal Humbert; the legates were then subjected to a similar sentence issued by the synod of Constantinople ... We must recognize today that the sentences were directed at particular persons and not at the churches, and were not aiming at breaking ecclesial communion between the sees of Rome and Constantinople."[2]

It is clear from this text of the "lifting of the anathemas" that the authors were aware of the rather accidental character of the 1054 events. In 1054 no schism occurred between the churches as such. Humbert's text includes "the supporters of (Cerularius') folly" under the condemnation, but in the same text he considers the emperor of Constantinople and the citizens as "very Christian and orthodox." In any case, his "bull" of excommunication exceeded his powers as legate, and was apparently null and void in the first place.

It was therefore rather easy for Paul VI and Athenagoras to express "regret" about the "offensive words" of 1054 and "to lift from the memory and the midst of the Church the sentences of excommunication." And it is good that they did so. However, they did not put an end to the schism itself.

What then is the nature of the schism and when did it occur?

All historians admit today that East and West parted ways through a *progressive* estrangement, which coincided with the equally *progressive* growth of papal authority. Theologians held centuries-long discussions on such issues as the trinitarian dogma (the *filioque* question), and the issues were important ones. However, no solution of the

[2]*Tomos Agapes, Vatican-Phanar* [1958-1970] (Rome, Istanbul, 1971), p. 127.

debate could be reached until the two sides reached agreement not only on the substance (which was difficult
enough) but also on who was to sanction the agreement and
on what basis.

Elements of the estrangement appeared even in the fourth
century, when a certain polarization in trinitarian theology
already existed along with an incipient ecclesiological conflict. On the one hand, the West attributed a particular
authority to the so-called "apostolic sees" and recognized the
Roman see as the only "see of Peter"; on the other hand, in
the East "apostolic sees" (local churches tracing their origin
to an apostle) were so numerous, that they could not practically pretend to any particular authority on that basis.[3]
However, no one in the East raised any objection of principle
against the rise of the "ecumenical patriarchate" of Constantinople, the imperial capital, based exclusively upon empirical
factors quite independent of any "apostolicity."[4]

Clearly the ecclesiological polarization involved in the
estrangement of East and West was connected with a gradually diverging understanding of the *local church*, i.e. the
eucharistic community headed by a bishop and presbyters and
including the people of God. Relationships between the local
churches were seen in the East as based upon their *identity*
of faith and total ontological equality, with "primacies"
(metropolitanates, patriarchates, etc.) emerging on an empirical basis conditioned and controlled only by the consensus
of all the churches. In the West there was an insistence on
"apostolicity," particularly on the apostolicity of Rome alone
because it was the only "apostolic" see of the West. This
led to an idea of leadership by divine election, since Christ
and not the Church had chosen and appointed the apostles
and selected Peter for a special role in the Church. But when
the debate started in the thirteenth century the Byzantine side
insisted upon the idea of a *succession of Peter in each local*

[3]This point is brilliantly shown in F. Dvornik, *The Legend of the
Apostle Andrew and the Idea of Apostolicity in Byzantium* (Cambridge,
Mass.: Harvard University Press, 1968).

[4]On this theme see also Dvornik's *Byzantium and the Roman Primacy*
(New York: Fordham University Press, 1966), esp. pp. 27-58.

*church* in person of the bishop, the "high-priest" and teacher at the eucharistic gathering.[5] This idea had already been expressed in the doctrine of the *cathedra Petri* of St. Cyprian of Carthage in the third century.

The initial estrangement grew progressively deeper and was enhanced by political and cultural factors. If one excepts Pope Leo I and the important role his "Letter to Flavian" played at the Council of Chalcedon (451), the Roman Church had no decisive influence upon the trinitarian and christological debates raging in the East. Rome's doctrinal authority was acknowledged, but it was the conciliar agreement of the episcopate which was seen as the highest expression of ecclesial authority. This authority, however, was not juridically automatic, and there were many examples of "pseudo-councils." Conciliar authority fits the biblical category of divine "signs." These are addressed to the Christian community as a whole, but do not deprive it of the responsibility to "discern" truth and falsehood.

The Crusades, and particularly the attack of Constantinople which occurred in 1204, are frequently seen by historians as the real beginning of the schism. It is obvious that the establishment of a *parallel Latin hierarchy*, and particularly of a Latin patriarchate of Constantinople, made the schism clearly evident. In any case, after the Gregorian Reforms the papacy considered itself the ultimate authority in Christendom. Challenge to that authority was seen as a schismatic and heretical act. The Easterners, meanwhile, seem to have maintained longer the idea that, in spite of all the crimes committed by the Crusaders, the Latin West remained a part of the Christian *oikoumene*. This can be said not only of the "Latinophrones," who constantly pushed the weakening empire of the Palaeologoi towards a "political" union with Rome in order to secure help against the Turks, but also of more conservative Orthodox circles as

[5]On this dimension of Orthodox ecclesiology, see J. D. Zizioulas, "The Eucharistic Community and the Catholicity of the Church," in J. Meyendorff and J. McLelland, eds., *The New Man: An Orthodox and Reformed Dialogue* (New Brunswick, N. J.: Agora Books, 1973), pp. 132-148; also on the idea of Peter's succession in Byzantium, J. Meyendorff *et al.*, *The Primacy of Peter in the Orthodox Church* (London: Faith Press, 1963).

well. These circles, taking quite seriously theological issues, particularly the addition of the *filioque* to the Creed by the Latins, considered that a council of union at which these differences could be openly debated and resolved, was a necessary pre-condition for the healing of the schism.[6]

Throughout the fourteenth century the debates between East and West centered around the idea of a *council*. But was a council to precede union, as the Byzantines wanted, or was an act of "penance," of "return," necessary as a precondition? The popes maintained the latter position until the papacy itself began to be challenged by the conciliarist movement of the West. Proclaiming the supremacy of the council over the pope, the Council of Constance made the previously held papal position untenable, and eventually led to a "union council" in Ferrara-Florence (1438-1439). Ironically the Council of Florence ended in a double tragedy, the end of conciliarism in the West[7] and the final schism between the East and West. Indeed, the Decree of Florence[8] was bound to provoke a reaction. It imposed upon an exhausted and despairing Greek delegation the traditional positions of the Latin West on the *filioque* and Purgatory; and last but not least, it defined the position of the Roman Pontiff as implying "full power (*plena potestas*) to feed, rule, and govern the universal Church." Most of the Greek delegates who signed the decree, later retracted their endorsements. The Church of Russia rejected Metropolitan Isidore, one of the architects of the union. After the Turkish conquest the patriarchate of Constantinople officially placed Latin Christians in the "second category" of heretics, to be accepted into the Church by Chrismation in accordance with canon 95 of the Quinisext Council (692).

All these well-known events are to be kept in mind if the "lifting of anathemas" of 1965 is to be understood in its true light. Clearly, the end of the schism will require much

[6]See J. Meyendorff, "Projets de concile oecuménique en 1367," in *Dumbarton Oaks Papers* vol. 14 (1960).

[7]Cf. J. Gill, *The Council of Florence* (Cambridge, 1959), p. vii.

[8]H. Denzinger and C. Rahner, *Enchiridion Symbolorum* (Freiburg, 1952), pp. 252-253.

more than this symbolic act. In particular the acceptance by both sides of a common frame of reference in terms of church *authority* will be needed.

I would like to point out one major past event which could serve as an important reference in this respect: the great Council of Constantinople held in 879-80, which is even designated in some Byzantine sources as the "council of union." A proper understanding of it today could contribute substantially to resolving the conflicting views of authority in East and West. Following such ecclesiologically significant events as the mutual excommunications of Pope Nicholas I and Patriarch Photius, and a first round of polemics concerning the *filioque* clause, this council sealed a reconciliation between Pope John VIII and Patriarch Photius. Until recently it was assumed that Pope John VIII disavowed his legates when they returned from the East, and that the schism continued. The work of F. Dvornik and other modern scholars has shown that this was not the case,[9] and that not only Photius and John VIII, but also their several successors remained faithful to the council's achievement.

The council reached two major decisions.

(1)   On the level of discipline, the two churches would recognize each other as supreme instances in their respective spheres. There would be no papal "jurisdiction" in the East (canon 1), but the traditional honorary primacy of Rome would be recognized, as well as the traditional territorial limits of the Roman patriarchate.

(2)   On the level of doctrinal teaching, the council maintains unity of faith, through a reaffirmation of the original text of the Creed of Nicaea-Constantinople. "Additions" to the text are explicitly condemned. The *filioque* is clearly implied in the conciliar decree, but the authority of the pope is not directly involved, since the addition at that time was not yet used in Rome itself but only in Frankish lands and in Spain.

What is the significance of these decisions?

[9] See particularly F. Dvornik, *The Photian Schism: History and Legend* (Cambridge, 1948).

The texts themselves call the council "holy and ecumenical." Indeed all the criteria of ecumenicity accepted for
previous councils were present in 879-880: imperial convocation and representation of the five patriarchates including
Rome. In Byzantine canonical collections the decrees of
879-880 always follow those of the other seven ecumenical
councils. Byzantine authors often mention the assembly as
the "eighth" ecumenical council. This is the case, for example, with such eminent and representative authors as
Nicholas Cabasilas[10] and Symeon of Thessalonica.[11] However, this usage was not general. Some Byzantine authors
considered the "seven councils" as *de facto* limited in number by the sacredness of the number seven. Others respected
the Latin reluctance concerning the council.

Dvornik shows[12] that in the West the council of 879-880
was recognized, if not as ecumenical, at least as a competent
authority sanctioned by Rome. It was seen as reestablishing
church unity by annulling the previously held "Ignatian"
council (869-870) which had deposed Photius.[13] Only at the
end of the eleventh century did the Gregorian Reform restore
the authority of the "Ignatian" council. The Gregorian Reforms recognized themselves in the *Acts* of this council
which (so they thought) affirmed the authority of the pope
over the Byzantine patriarch and the civil power of the emperors. But between 880 and 1100, for more than two centuries, the East and the West, in spite of the other differences
which separated them, recognized the legitimacy of the agreement between John VIII and Photius sealed at St. Sophia in
880.

Clearly, the rather tardy introduction of the Ignatian
council of 869-870 into the list of "ecumenical" councils does

[10]Preamble to the works of Cabasilas, Migne P.G. 149, col. 679.

[11]*Dial.* 19, P.G. 155, col. 97.

[12]*Photian Schism*, pp. 309-330.

[13]In a recent book Daniel Stiernon tries to reestablish the authority of this
"Ignatian council," which is listed as "eighth ecumenical" in the presently
accepted Roman Catholic lists (*Constantinople IV* [Paris, Editions de
l'Orante: 1967], pp. 199-230). But the famous *Decretum* of Ivo Chartres,
published in 1094, witnesses unquestionably to the rehabilitation of Photius
by John VIII, as it was then recognized in the West.

present the Roman concept of authority with a problem. Can it be reconciled with such an obvious break in continuity? It is interesting, however, that at least once the issue was successfully by-passed. During the fourth and fifth sessions of the council in Ferrara on October 20 and 24, 1438, Cardinal Cesarini and Andrew of Rhodes, the main spokesmen for the Latin side, invoked the authority of the "eighth council," meaning the Ignatian council of 869-870. They immediately had to face a blunt *non possumus* from Mark of Ephesus, the Greek spokesman, who expressly appealed to the formal annulment of this council under Pope John VIII.[14] By common accord the ticklish issue was buried and the Council of Florence became the "eighth" council. The Latin side thus implicitly accepted a return to the situation which preceded the Gregorian Reform.

I am now coming to an idea which in my opinion might be decisive in solving the problem of authority between Rome and Orthodoxy. Would it not be possible today *jointly to recognize the Photian council of 879-880 as ecumenical?*

An act of this kind would certainly go much farther than the purely symbolic "lifting of the anathemas" of 1054. It would imply a return to the situation which existed for more than two centuries. For the Orthodox such an act would require the agreement of all the local Orthodox churches; and it would mean that union is really based on identity of faith, expressed in the common creed. For tradition-minded Rome it would not be a simple abdication of authority, but a return to a situation solemnly sanctioned by a predecessor of the present pope.

The nature of the schism being what it is, it is clear that symbolic gestures and ceremonial meetings are quite insufficient to overcome the existing division. What is needed is a union of minds and a basic agreement on institutional forms of unity. The council of 879-880 accomplished both.

---

[14]*Concilium Florentinum. Documenta et Scriptores. Series B.* Vol. V, fasc. I, *Acta Graeca* (Rome, 1952), p. 90-91, 135.

## II. *What happened in the 'sixties?*

We have described the various statements and encounters between the pope and the patriarch of Constantinople which took place in the 'sixties as having been essentially of a *symbolic* nature. All symbols can be wrongly interpreted. It has been said, for example, that the spectacular character of the encounters and the ambiguity of the documents gave the mistaken impression that union was imminent and that doctrinal obstacles existed only in the minds of a few reactionary theologians. It has also been said that the ecclesiastical diplomacy which prepared and realized the encounters was aimed at projecting the false image of an Orthodox "papacy," parallel to the Roman one, and one must say that an uninformed Western public may have occasionally thought that the ecumenical patriarch was the Eastern equivalent of a pope. On the Orthodox side the sceptics found consolation in the fact that the patriarch was not invested with any official Pan-Orthodox mandate and that he was neither speaking nor acting for the whole Church.

It would be unfortunate, however, if these critiques, sometimes justified, of the papal and patriarchal diplomacies were to neutralize completely the real importance of certain gestures and certain words. The events may still bring about consequences which will transcend our immediate reactions. It would be impossible, for example, even to think about a joint acceptance of the council of 879-880, if the atmosphere created by Vatican II and by the meetings between Paul VI and Athenagoras were not with us.

There are two realities which merit particular attention because they are directly relevant to the central issue of authority.

(1) The public *image*, witnessed by the entire world, of a pope appearing in Istanbul and in Rome as a *brother* and therefore ontologically an *equal* of another bishop, cannot be reduced to mere diplomacy or protocol. Of course, the well-known definitions of papal supremacy were in no way denied, but they were not expressed in any way either. Facing the Orthodox, the pope presented himself to them

in a way perfectly compatible with the function of *primus inter pares* ("first among equals") which the Orthodox have recognized in him in the past. This attitude of Paul VI reverses a thousand-year-old tradition which required that the authority of the supreme pontiff be scrupulously preserved under any circumstances, and particularly in his relations with the East where the existence of a center of opposition to Roman centralism was well known. The rupture of that tradition evident in the case of Pope Paul raises a general ecclesiological question. If the pope's power over the Latin episcopate is traditionally justified by the notion of a "universal jurisdiction" by divine right, is there not a contradiction between that position and the fraternal embrace exchanged with Athenagoras, whose episcopal dignity, magisterial authority and patriarchal jurisdiction were strictly independent of Rome?

It appears, at least to this author, that papal power, as defined by Vatican I, either is universal or it is not. It is difficult to understand why the bishops of France, Polynesia, America or Africa should profit from a divinely established papal "immediate" jurisdiction, while the bishops of Greece, Russia or the Middle East would not.

There are still no clear answers to these questions, and perhaps such answers would be difficult to conceptualize. It is also obvious that inside Roman Catholicism a diversity of trends and a variety of pressure groups exist. Paradoxically, those groups which are most opposed to Roman centralism are not always sympathetic to the values which Orthodoxy represents: faithfulness to apostolic doctrine and a sacramental approach to church polity. It remains, however, that the pope and patriarch, sitting side by side and addressing each other as equals, have established a precedent which needs a theological and ecclesial reception and interpretation. The symbol needs to be given a substantial content.

(2)  On July 25, 1967, in Istanbul the pope handed to Patriarch Athenagoras the brief *Anno ineunte*, which aims at expressing the relationship between Rome and Constantinople using the traditional Orthodox concept of "sister churches." The text recognizes that the term is appropriate

to describe the relations as they existed "for centuries" and then it continues: "Now, after a long period of division and reciprocal misunderstanding, it occurs, by the grace of God, that our churches recognize each other as sisters once more."[15] The basis for such a recognition is found in the mystery of the sacramental presence of Christ. This mystery is present in each local church, and therefore, "communion (between our churches), though imperfect, already exists."

This text has certain implications.

(1) The rapprochement between East and West must be understood as a progressive mutual recognition of local churches, and not as a return to Roman "obedience." It is certain that this method basically corresponds to the Orthodox approach to the ecumenical task in general, although Orthodox rapprochement with Rome possess a much more solid ecclesiological basis than the contacts with the Protestants. One wonders, however, whether this method can be really consistent with those definitions of Roman primacy which are based on the exclusive "Petrine" ministry of the pope. Actually, at the very beginning of the brief *Anno inneunte* itself, the pope is designated as "bishop of the Roman Church and head of the universal Church,"[16] a title which clearly reflects an ecclesiology which the Orthodox consider as quite incompatible with their own. Isn't there a contradiction in the brief itself?

(2) The doctrinal definitions made by the Latin Church and traditionally rejected by the Orthodox—the addition of the *filioque* to the text of the Creed, the Council of Trent, the dogma of the Immaculate Conception of Mary (1854)— are somehow set in parentheses. Their rejection by the Orthodox does not preclude "an almost full" communion. The implication of the brief *Anno inneunte* has recently been reinforced by the text of a letter of Pope Paul VI to Cardinal Willebrands, dated October 5, 1974. The cardinal was the

---

[15]*Tomos Agapes*, p. 390.

[16]To avoid embarrassing the Orthodox, the Greek text of the brief translates *caput* ("head") as *hegoumenos* ("leader"). This diplomatic mistranslation only emphasizes the ambiguity of the thought lying behind the text of the brief.

papal legate at the celebrations of the 700th anniversary of the Council of Lyons (1274) which solemnly defined the theology of the *filioque* and accepted the unionist confession of faith signed by the Byzantine Emperor Michael VIII Palaeologus. The remarkable thing about this papal letter is that it recognizes that the council gave no "possibility to the Greek Church of expressing itself freely," and that "a unity achieved in this way could not be accepted completely by the mentality of the Eastern Christians." Even more significantly, the pope calls the Council of Lyons "the sixth of the general synods held in the Western world," and *not* an "ecumenical council." Can the same then be said of Trent, Vatican I, and Vatican II? If so, a really important step, modifying the previously held concept of papal authority, seems to have been taken.

In any case, the texts seem to imply that the Latin dogmas, so solemnly proclaimed in the past, should not be considered as possessing a universal validity, and therefore should not constitute an obstacle to union. If this is really so, the authority of the Roman Church, which previously committed itself so heavily behind these dogmas, should also be seen in a new light. However, a canonical and sacramental union which did not presuppose the solution of the problems raised by these Latin definitions, would raise more acutely the question of theological pluralism in a united Church. Certainly, there is nothing new in considering certain practices and doctrines as *theologoumena*, i.e. positions taken by individual theologians without formal ecclesial sanction. Liturgical and theological pluralism are both unavoidable and desirable in the One Church. But this admissible pluralism is not an end in itself, and should not be used to justify doctrinal relativism as such, or to cover up serious doctrinal conflicts. A *theologoumenon* cannot be imposed as obligatory doctrine, but everyone has the right to reject it if he sees it as erroneous. The later Latin dogmas would certainly be seen in this last category by the Orthodox. They were not merely signs of pluralism, but were occasions for centuries-long conflicts. Can one have unity without solving these problems first?

Another set of questions raised by texts like *Anno inneunte* and the papal letter to Cardinal Willebrands is also directly connected with the issue of authority. The texts certainly make a step in the direction of the Orthodox if they really imply that Latin medieval and modern doctrinal developments are not obligatory for the Easterners because the Eastern "sister-churches" did not receive them. But if these doctrines failed to obtain the support of the East, does this not mean that they should be treated with at least some reservations in the West as well? Can the authority of the doctrinal definitions of Lyons, Florence, Trent and Vatican I be limited geographically? On the other hand, the Orthodox certainly should feel some responsibility for the West as well, where some of these "dogmas" have also provoked conflicts. And finally, what is the "East" and what is the "West" in this last quarter of the twentieth century?

The remarkable change of atmosphere witnessed recently in the relations between the two churches, and the quite real efforts made by Popes John XXIII and Paul VI to meet the Orthodox in the question of Church authority, require a balanced theological evaluation which must show whether the questions raised above have received at least the beginning of an answer.

### III. *The ambiguity of the present situation*

The question of authority has stood for centuries in the very center of the issues between East and West. Writing in the middle of the last century the Russian lay theologian A. S. Khomiakov defined the issue in the form of a somewhat romantic overstatement, which, however, remains quite suggestive today. "The Church is not an authority, just as God is not an authority and Christ is not an authority, since authority is something external to us. The Church is not an authority, I say, but the Truth, and at the same time the inner life of the Christian, since God, Christ, the Church, live in him with a life more real than the heart which is beating in his breast and the blood flowing in his veins. But they are alive in him only insofar as he himself is living by the ecumenical life of love and unity, i.e. by the life of the Church." Khomiakov's main reproach to the West is that it has transformed authority into external power: the *magisterium* in Roman Catholicism, Scripture in Protestantism. In both cases, he concludes "the premises are identical."[17]

Khomiakov's notion of an "internal" knowledge of the Truth, independent of "external" criteria and authorities, would appear to be pure romantic subjectivism if it were read outside of the context of the Greek patristic understanding of God and man. For the Greek Fathers knowledge of God is based on the idea of communion, transfiguration, and deification of man. It implies the theory of the "spiritual senses," i.e. an utterly personal experience of the Living God, made accessible through the sacramental, communal life in the Body of Christ.[18] This gnosiology does not suppress "authorities" and "criteria," but it conceives them as clearly *internal* to the Christian experience. They furnish an authentication which is incomprehensible to anyone who has not first personally accepted the validity and tasted to the reality of the experience.

The experience is that of Truth itself, not simply of a means for attaining the Truth. It involves the "uncreated" and divine presence of God in man through the Holy Spirit. It is the Truth therefore that authenticates authority, and not vice versa. It is precisely this understanding of authority which made the East resist so stubbornly against accepting the institution of papacy as the criterion of Truth. Because of this the Orthodox reaffirm consistently that it is the faith of Peter which conditions primacy, while primacy itself

[17]*Quelques mots d'un chrétien orthodoxe sur les confessions occidentales* (Paris, 1853), reprinted in *L'Eglise latine et le protestantisme au point de vue de l'Eglise d'Orient. Recueil d'articles sur des questions religieuses ecrits à différents époques et à différentes occasions* (Lausanne et Vevey, 1872), pp. 36-37; Engl. tr. in A. Schmemann, ed., *Ultimate Questions* (New York: Holt, Rinehart and Winston, 1965), pp. 50-51.

[18]The classical book on Eastern Christian gnosiology is by V. Lossky, *The Mystical Theology of the Eastern Church* (London: James Clarke, 1957); see also, by the same author, *Vision of God* (London: Faith Press, 1963), and our own *Byzantine Theology: Historical Trends and Doctrinal Themes* (New York: Fordham University Press, 1974).

is not a guarantee of infallibility. Here, in fact, is the traditional issue between Rome and Orthodoxy.

We have shown above that the moves made recently by
Rome towards conciliarity, towards the concept of "sister-
churches," and towards limiting the significance of unilateral
Roman decisions on faith, must be seen as significant ecumenical progress. The *ambiguity* appears, however, as soon
as these moves are applied to practice. The traditional re-
liance of Western Christianity upon authority in matters of
religion creates a religious void wherever authority weakens
or disappears. Deprived of the security provided by the
familiar authority structures (the teaching Church or the in-
errant Bible) and suspicious of anything which was associated with it—including paradoxically, the liturgical Mystery—
Western Christianity moves in the directions which estrange it
most from Orthodoxy: humanistic activism and secularism.
But then, as a reaction against these trends, the old clerical
forms of post-Tridentine Roman Catholicism and conservative Protestant fundamentalism reappear, stronger than
ever.

Clearly, all this may be seen as an oversimplification, but
it does reflect the feeling of many Orthodox, whose reaction
is to withdraw from the ecumenical "adventures" altogether
and simply to enjoy, on their own, the beautiful foretaste of
the kingdom to come in the Orthodox liturgy. This is a natural reaction for those who cannot identify with either pole
of contemporary Western Christianity.

It is certainly not my intention to finish on this pessimistic
note. I do not believe that withdrawal from dialogue is anything but a renunciation of one's "catholic" responsibility.
But I do want to emphasize the fact that between the conciliar ecclesiology of Orthodoxy and the infallibilism of
Vatican I the issue was indeed that of "authority," which
could be discussed as such. But since the 'sixties, the issue
has shifted. A discussion of papal primacy and church authority in general has become impossible without relating it to
the very *content* of the Christian Gospel. For if this content is not guaranteed by an "authority" any more, it must
be preserved through a corporate knowledge and commit-

ment of the whole Church. The very goal of Christian life, and indeed of the ecumenical movement, is to make the full Truth of the Christian experience always accessible in the Christian community. A united commitment to that experience makes the Church truly one.

# 5

# The Catholicity of
# the Church*

The term "catholicity" is comparatively recent in origin.
The patristic and credal tradition knows only the adjective
*catholic* and proclaims our faith in the "catholic Church"
(καθολικὴ ἐκκλησία). To speak of "catholicity" reflects
a preoccupation with abstract ideas, while the real object of
theological concern is the *Church*. Perhaps if the Fathers had
developed—as does modern theology—a special branch of
theological science called "ecclesiology," they would have
come to use the term "catholicity" as an abstraction or a
generalization of the adjective "catholic," just as they spoke
of "deity" (θεότης), "humanity" (ἀνθρωπότης), etc.,
when they were defining the hypostatic union. But it is a
fact that patristic thought has somehow avoided speaking of
the "marks" of the Church *in abstracto*. Neither was there
among the Fathers a tendency to "hypostasize" and "objec-
tify" the Church itself. When they speak of the *catholic*
Church, the Fathers say, first of all, that it is the "Body of
Christ" and the "Temple of the Spirit." The four adjectives
which describe the Church in our Creed, including the adjective "catholic," all refer to the *divine* nature of the Church
as the presence of Christ and the Spirit in the world. In the
patristic period the Church was not itself an object of specu-
lation or even of controversy (except in the second and third
centuries), *but it was the living context of all theology.* As

*Originally published in *St. Vladimir's Theological Quarterly* vol. 17: 1/2
(1973), pp. 5-18.

we all know, this is unfortunately no longer the case. In the ecumenical movement the nature and identity of the Church is understood differently by the various Christian groups. In contemporary Orthodox theology itself a peculiar compartmentalization of concepts and areas (generally imported from the West) has led to a divorce between Church and theology—a divorce which explains why both Church and theology are in a deep crisis.

One cannot over-emphasize how urgent it is for us Orthodox to recover the sense of a "churchly" theology which is truly Christ-centered and Spirit-centered, and which implies unity between life and dogma, liturgy and theology, love and truth. The credibility of our message to our own youth, to other Christians, and to a world which has lost Christ but is often still searching for Him, depends on such a recovery. Our common confession of faith in the "catholic Church" alone can contribute to this urgent need.

Three areas where the implications of "catholicity" are of crucial importance are the structure of the Church, its relations with other Christians, and its mission to the world. The traditional, and the only possible, Orthodox approach to "catholicity" is rooted in the fullness of God's trinitarian life and is therefore a *gift* of God to men, thus making the Church the "Church of God." This gift implies man's responsibility. God's gift is not simply a treasury to be kept, or a predestination to be enjoyed. It is a seed planted in the world and in history, a seed which man, as a free and responsible being, is called upon to cultivate so that the catholicity of the Church may be realized every day in the ever-changing conditions of the life of the world.

There is a remarkable consensus among Orthodox theologians at international meetings as long as they affirm and describe the divine, eternal, and absolute truths of Orthodox theology about God, Christ, and the Church, even if they differ in temperament and in methodology. In this fundamental agreement there is a great security, and it is good and proper for all of us to rejoice quite sincerely in this meeting of minds and agreement in faith. Here and here only lies the hope for the future.

However, is it not equally obvious that when it comes to the practical application of these divine truths which unite us all the Orthodox Church shows an image of division and inconsistency? This gap between "theory" and "practice," between our "faith" and our "works," is there to be seen by outsiders as well as by ourselves. It is fortunate that we are not always totally devoid of a sense of humor, for I have often heard at Orthodox meetings—even on the hierarchical level—the half-cynical remark that "Orthodoxy is the right faith held by the wrong people."

Of course the gap between divine perfection and the deficiencies of sinful men is nothing new in the life of the Church. It is at all times appropriate to consider, along with Nicholas Berdyaev, the "dignity of Christianity" as well as the "indignity of Christians." However, in our present situation there is something particularly tragic in the serenity with which we so often proclaim that we are indeed the "true catholic Church," and at the same time continue our games which *we know* are inconsistent with what we believe the Church to be.

It is urgent that we recover our *moral* consistency. To provide guidelines for such a recovery is the primary task of theology, but it must be something more than a purely academic pursuit if it is to serve the Church of Christ and to proclaim divine truth to the world which God created. It is indeed urgent, because in the midst of our clergy and faithful one begins to sense a mental *désarroi* which leads to doubtful escape-channels: sectarianism, pseudo-spiritualism, or cynical relativism. All these escapes are attractive to some because they are easy solutions, reducing the mystery of the Church to human dimensions and providing a measure of illusory security to the mind. But if we agree that these are deviations from the "narrow path" of catholicity, we should be able to define not only what catholicity is as God's gift, but also what it means to be an Orthodox Catholic today. Our Orthodox Church should be the witness to its own catholicity. When it succeeds in bridging the gap between "theory" and "practice," theology immediately becomes the theology of the Church, as it was in the time of St. Basil and

St. John Chrysostom, and not simply a "clanging cymbal" (κύμβαλον ἀλαλάζον—I Cor. 13:1).

## I. The Structure of the Church

When we say that the Church is "catholic," we affirm a quality or a "mark" of the Church which is to be realized in the individual life of each Christian, in the life of the local community or "Church," and in the manifestations of the Church's universal unity. Since we are now concerned with the structure of the Church, I will speak of the local and universal dimensions of "catholicity" in the Christian community.

(a)    Orthodox ecclesiology is based on the notion that a local Christian community, gathered in the name of Christ, presided over by the bishop, and celebrating the eucharistic meal, is indeed the "catholic Church" and the Body of Christ—not a "fragment" of the Church, or only a part of the Body. This is so because the Church is "catholic" through Christ, not through its human membership. "Where Christ is, there is the catholic Church" (Ign., *Smyrn.* 8:2). This local dimension of catholicity, which is one of the foundations of our theology of the episcopate, of our understanding of the councils and of tradition, is probably accepted by all Orthodox theologians and has even won some positive recognition outside Orthodoxy in the past years. It has important practical consequences for the life of the local churches. These consequences are often called "canonical" but in fact they transcend the legal aspect of the canonical texts. The authority of the canons actually lies in the theological and dogmatic truths about the Church which the canons are called to express and protect.

Thus the catholicity of the local Church implies in particular that it encompass *all* Orthodox Christians in each place. This is not only a "canonical" but a doctrinal requirement as well, and a necessary implication of catholicity which becomes obvious as soon as one recognizes *Christ* as the ultimate criterion of Church structure. It is also an expression of the basic Gospel precept about "love for our neighbor."

The Gospel does not call us to love only our friends, or only to preserve our ethnic ties, or to love humanity in general, but *to love our neighbors,* i.e. those whom God has chosen to meet us in our earthly existence. The local "catholic" Church of Christ is the gathering of those who not only love each other as neighbors, but also are fellow citizens of Christ's Kingdom and recognize together the full significance of love as expressed by their only Head, their only Lord, their only Master—Christ. Those who do so become together members of one catholic Church of Christ, as it is manifested in the local eucharistic assembly under the leadership of the one local bishop. If they do not act in this manner they betray the commandment of love, obscure the meaning of eucharistic unity, and ignore the catholicity of the Church.

These facts of our faith are quite obvious, and equally obvious is our reluctance to take this Christian faith seriously enough to draw the appropriate conclusions, especially here in America. The usual reference to the existence of liturgical communion between the various territorially overlapping "jurisdictions" as a sufficient expression of their unity is obviously improper. Eucharistic ecclesiology, which properly understood is the only true Orthodox ecclesiology, shows that eucharistic unity is to be realized in life, reflected in Church structure, and in general is to provide the Christ-centered pattern on which the entire life of the Church as such is based. This is the true significance of the liturgy.

It is, therefore, our duty as theologians and as Orthodox Christians to recognize that our systematic reluctance to accept our mission as witnesses to the Church's catholicity, and our preference for permanent ethnic divisions, are betrayals of catholicity.

(b)   The "catholicity" of the local Church also provides a theological substance to the Orthodox doctrine of the various ministries, and particularly that of the episcopate. As we all know, apostolic succession is bestowed upon the bishops as heads and pastors of concrete local churches. Orthodox ecclesiology is faithful to the ancient tradition of the Church, which never knew "bishops in general," but only bishops of concrete, stable communities. The entire Orthodox insistence on the ontological equality of all bishops among themselves is based on the principle that each one of them presides over the *same catholic Church* in a given place, and that no local Church can be more "catholic" than another. No bishop can therefore be more a bishop than his brothers presiding over the same Church elsewhere.

But what then about so many of our "titular" bishops? How can they be spokesmen for the "catholic" Church if their episcopate is devoid of concrete pastoral responsibility for clergy and laity in a given place? How can we Orthodox Christians defend the episcopate as belonging to the very *esse* of the Church (as we always do at ecumenical gatherings) when the episcopate has often become a simple "dignity" bestowed upon individuals for the sake of prestige? What is the authority of synods and councils composed of "titular" bishops?

(c)   There is also a *universal* dimension to catholicity. To follow the standard concepts accepted since St. Cyprian of Carthage, each local catholic Church is centered on the *cathedra Petri* occupied by its local bishop, but since there is everywhere only *one* catholic Church, there is also only *one episcopate* (*episcopatus unus est*). The particular function of the bishop consists both in being the pastor of his local Church and in carrying a responsibility for the universal communion of all the churches. This is the theological meaning of episcopal conciliarity, and it is an ontologically required element in the episcopal consecration, which presupposes a gathering of all the bishops of a given province representing the one episcopate of the universal Church. Episcopal conciliarity is also the highest witness to apostolic truth, the most authentic authority in doctrinal and canonical matters. It has two traditional expressions, regional and universal. In each case it requires a structure, an organizational channel through which conciliarity becomes a permanent feature of church life. Hence the appearance early in church history of many regional "primacies" and of one universal primacy. Obviously, the basic principle of Orthodox ecclesiology, which affirms the full catholicity of the local Church and therefore the ontological *identity* of the episcopal ministry everywhere, can admit only primacies *inter pares*; and the location of these primacies can only be determined through a consensus of the local churches (*ex consensu ecclesiae*). The essential function of all "primacies" consists in assuring a regular and orderly practice of episcopal conciliarity on the regional and universal levels.

The above principles are, I believe, uncontroversial and admitted everywhere in the Orthodox world. But what happens in reality? The heads of our various "autocephalous" churches exercise their "primacies" in rough conformity with canonical tradition as chairmen and leaders of local synods of bishops. Most of them, however, are not "regional" but *ethnic* primates. To a large extent the ethnic element has replaced the regional and the territorial principles of church structure, and this evolution must be considered as nothing else but a *secularization* of the Church. The phenomenon of "national churches" is certainly not entirely new. There is a fully legitimate degree to which the Church can identify itself with national ethos and tradition and assume some responsibility for the society in which it exists. The Orthodox East has always encouraged the assumption by the Church of those elements of national tradition which could contribute to the progress of Christianity in each given nation. However, since the secularization of nationalism which occurred everywhere in Europe in the nineteenth century, the scale of values was reversed. The "nation" and its interests began to be considered as ends in themselves, and instead of guiding their nations to Christ most Orthodox churches accepted *de facto* control by secular national interests. The principle of "autocephaly"[1] began to be understood as total self-sufficiency and indepedence, and the relations between "autocephalous" churches were conceived in terms borrowed from secular international law. In fact, however, the *only*— I say, the *only*—ecclesiologically and canonically legitimate

[1] I use the term "autocephaly" in its modern sense. In the Byzantine canonical texts the adjective "autocephalous" most frequently designated individual "archdioceses" which were not dependent upon a regional mettropolitan and his synod, but were appointed either by a patriarch or by the emperor directly.

meaning of "autocephaly" is to give a group of dioceses the right to elect its bishops without any interference from a "higher" primate, i.e. a patriarch, archbishop, or metropolitan. "Autocephaly" presupposes conformity with the universal structure of the Orthodox Church. Historically and canonically, several ethnic elements can be grouped in one "autocephaly," and a single "nation" may comprise several autocephalous groups of dioceses. Not "autocephaly" but *territorial unity* is the fundamental requirement of Orthodox ecclesiology.

An equally dangerous confusion has occurred in relation to universal "primacy." Since the world episcopate is *one*, as also the universal Church is one, holy tradition has always recognized the ecclesiological necessity of having a co-ordinating center of communion and common action. This service of unity was fulfilled in apostolic times by the Church of Jerusalem. In the second century there was already a general consensus for some preeminence of the Church of Rome. There was also a very early polarization of minds between the East and West concerning the criteria which were to be employed in recognizing and locating universal primacy. The Orthodox East has always considered that no mystical significance can be attached to the apostolicity of a Church, nor to any particular location, but that universal primacy (as well as the local primacies) should be established wherever this would be practical and convenient. Thus the Church of Constantinople was elevated to the second place after Rome "because it was the seat of the emperor and the senate" (canon 28 of Chalcedon), and after the schism this Church naturally assumed the universal primacy formerly enjoyed by the Roman pope. The reason for this elevation was the existence of a (nominally) universal Christian empire, of which Constantinople was the capital.

After the fall of Byzantium (1453), the reasons which had provoked the selection of Constantinople for the universal primacy disappeared. However, the Orthodox Church was now so much attached to its Byzantine forms and traditions that no one challenged Constantinople's primacy, especially since the Ecumenical Patriarchate was granted effective control over all the Orthodox Christians in the Ottoman Empire. Even Russia, which was out of Turkish control and whose tsars inherited the imperial title of the Byzantine *basileus*, never claimed universal primacy for its newly established patriarchate (1589). In fact, however, Constantinople was never again able to exercise direct and meaningful leadership outside the Ottoman borders. The sense of Orthodox unity suffered greatly from that situation. As the various Balkan states were receiving their political independence (Greece, Serbia, Rumania, Bulgaria, and later Albania), they fell out of the Phanar's ecclesiastical control and tended to ignore its leadership.

These are historical facts whose ultimate consequences we are facing today. But what about the ecclesiological necessity of having a world center of communion and action?

The answer to this question is found in Orthodox tradition. There is no doubt that such a center is needed, preferably with an international staff and the possibility for all local churches to maintain their permanent representatives on the spot. The Ecumenical Patriarch heading such a center should act as the real servant and initiator of Orthodox conciliarity. He should be independent from outside political pressures and should always act *ex consensu ecclesiae.*

The restoration of a church structure based on catholicity is not a matter of church politics, but of theology. Theologians are called to remind the Church that it is truly "catholic" only because it is Christ's, and that it can therefore manifest and realize its catholicity only by always accepting Christ as the ultimate and only pattern of its structure and order.

## II. Relations with other Christians

The doctrine of "catholicity" implies the legitimate possibility of cultural, liturgical, and theological diversity in the one Church of Christ. This diversity does not mean divergence and contradiction. The unity of the Church implies full unity of faith, of vision, of love. The unity of the one Body of Christ transcends all legitimate diversity. This unity,

we believe, is still possessed by the Orthodox Church, in spite
of all the personal or collective deficiencies of her members, and it is therefore the one true catholic Church. It is
Christ, not men, who gives the Church its catholicity and
unity, but it is up to us to *realize* unity and catholicity in
such a way as not to betray these great gifts of God's grace.

To be an "Orthodox Catholic" is, therefore, not only a
privilege but, first of all, a responsibility before God and
men. St. Paul, in his ministry, was able to be "a Jew with
the Jews" and "a Greek with the Greeks," but he also cas-
tigated these same "Jews" and "Greeks" when they were
refusing to form one single eucharistic community in
Corinth.

Diversity is not an end in itself. It is legitimate only when
it is at the same time overcome and transcended by unity in
the fullness of Christ's truth. It is to this unity that we
Orthodox must call non-Orthodox Christians, and our basic
claim again is that it is already found in the Orthodox
Church, and does not exist only on some invisible or pseudo-
"spiritual" level, of which all separated Christians equally
partake.

Unfortunately, the most serious obstacle to the credibility
of our claim is again the image presented by the Orthodox
Church: our inconsistency in even *attempting* to live up to
"catholicity"! Of this we gave several examples in reference
to church structure. Again I would emphasize that for the
time being an articulate witness about Orthodoxy always conflicts with observable facts in the concrete reality of the
Orthodox Church.

The difficulty of authentic witness is inherent in catholicity itself inasmuch as it is a *task* as well as a divine gift.
Catholicity implies active vigilance and discernment. It implies openness to all manifestations of God's creating and
redeeming power everywhere. The "catholic" Church rejoices
in whatever it finds of God's power, even outside its canonical
limits, because it is the Church of that same and one God
who is the origin of all good. In spite of all the errors and
heresies which we reject in the Western Christian tradition
it is clear that the Spirit of God has continued, even after the

schism, to inspire Western saints, thinkers, and millions of simple Christians. The grace of God did not suddenly depart when the schism occurred. The Orthodox Church has always recognized this, without in any way falling into relativism or ceasing to see itself as the only true catholic Church. For to be "catholic" means precisely to recognize everywhere that which is God-made and therefore basically "good," and to be ready to assume it as one's own. Catholicity rejects only that which is evil, or erroneous. We believe that the power of "discernment," the power of rejecting error and of accepting that which is authentic and right everywhere, is being exercised by the Holy Spirit in God's true Church. To quote St. Gregory of Nyssa, "Truth passes in the mean ... destroying each heresy, and yet accepting what is useful to it from each" (*Orat. Catech.* 3). This quotation should become our ecumenical motto! It is also particularly important for us, whom God has placed as witnesses for Orthodoxy in the midst of *Western* civilization.

The important biblical and canonical concepts of "discernment" (διάκρισις, esp. I Cor. 12:10 and Rom. 14:1) and "recognition" (in the meaning of the verb "to know," γιγνώσκειν, I John)—in both their positive and negative meanings—are the true foundation of an Orthodox approach to ecumenism. We betray the "catholicity" of the Church whenever we lose either the faculty of seeing that which is erroneous, or the loving and truly Christian faculty of rejoicing in that which is right and good. To cease to recognize the hand and presence of God wherever it appears and to adopt an attitude of pure negativism and defensiveness towards non-Orthodox Christians is not only a betrayal of catholicity, but also a form of neo-manicheism. Conversely, to lose the sense that error and heresy do exist and that they have a deadening effect on man, and to forget that the Church is built on the fullness of truth, is also a betrayal not only of Orthodox tradition, but also of the New Testament, upon which this tradition is built.

One of the present difficulties of our participation in the organized forms of the ecumenical movement resides in the recent commitment of many ecumenical agencies to modern theologies of "secularization," which are themselves based on long-standing Western tendencies to consider man as "autonomous" from God and his "secular" life as an end in itself. Some Orthodox react in a panicky and sectarian way while others fail to realize the seriousness of the situation, and comfortably use the advantages (often illusory) provided by their "image" as participants in the ecumenical movement. It is our responsibility as theologians to avoid these pitfalls and to provide the Church with guidelines for witness and action. At this point, therefore, our task in formulating an authentically Orthodox attitude towards ecumenism is inseparable from a theology of the "world"— another ambivalent scriptural term—which, in one sense, God "loved" and for whose life He gave His Son, and which, in another sense, we are being called to "hate."

## III. Catholicity and Mission

The Christian claim that Jesus is indeed the "Word of God," the Logos "through whom all things were made," is a universal claim which involves not only all men but also the entire cosmos. The Johannine identification between Christ and the Logos implies that Jesus is not just the "Savior of our souls." He is not only the carrier of a message limited to a peculiar field called "religion"; but in Him is the ultimate truth about the origin, the development, and the final destiny of *all things*. Hence His Church is necessarily the catholic Church (καθ' ὅλον) "referring to the whole."

We will probably all agree in rejecting the simplistic temptation to which Christians have often succumbed in the past, which consists in using the Bible as a reference book in physics or biology, or in claiming for the Church hierarchy the right of controlling scientific research and knowledge. These attitudes were based on a wrong interpretation of revelation and particularly on the identification of human words—through which God speaks in the Bible—with the unique, living, and personal Logos who speaks in His Church through the Holy Spirit.

We believe indeed that Jesus Christ is this personal divine Logos, in whom all the relative truths revealed in the Old Testament found their fulfillment, and in whom it is also possible to find the ultimate meaning of man's origin and destiny, on which science also furnishes us much important data. The goal of mission is indeed that all men would know Christ and in Him find communion with God. But knowledge of Christ and communion with God (that which was called *theosis* by the Fathers) are not communicated to men so that they may in any way *replace* man's knowledge of himself and of the cosmos, but in order to fulfill that knowledge, to give it a new meaning and a new creative dimension. Thus, the knowledge which comes from revelation, from Scripture and from Tradition, does not replace culture and science, but liberates the human mind from the secular or a-religious, i.e. from a necessarily one-sided approach to the reality of man and to the world.

These fundamental presuppositions have always served as the foundation of the Orthodox approach to the "world" and to mission. The tradition of using a vernacular language in worship itself implies that Christianity does not suppress indigenous cultures but assumes them into the united diversity of catholic tradition. In each case, however, this approach presents problems peculiar to each situation. The pluralistic and partly Christian culture of America, for example, is an unprecedented challenge to Orthodoxy, with which the now emerging American Orthodoxy must urgently cope. It requires a dynamic and creative approach. To seclude Orthodoxy in the ethnic ghettos which were instrumental in bringing the Orthodox faith to the new world is, on the one hand, a betrayal of catholicity; and on the other, it provides only an illusory protection against the overwhelming impact of American social reality. Neither does unconditional Americanization provide the right solution, because the "world" can never be accepted unconditionally into the Kingdom of God. It must first go through the paschal transformation and transfiguration through the cross and resurrection, and this indeed is a dynamic and creative process for which the Church needs the guidance of the Holy Spirit.

As we all know, contemporary theology of the "world" is in a state of great confusion. Many Protestants and some Roman Catholic theologians are pushing quite far the traditional Western concept of the "autonomy of the secular." The new secularist trend results not only in the view that the world is in a sense the only true *source* of revelation, but in the understanding of the world itself as paradoxically reduced to sociological categories. The destiny of man is interpreted almost exclusively in terms of economic development and social justice. The only competitor of this "social" bias in anthropology is Freudian pansexualism.

It seems to me that an articulate Orthodox reaction to these trends is one of our major tasks today, in the framework of the "catholic" witness of our Church. Without any triumphalism we can affirm and show that the Orthodox tradition concerning the nature of man is indeed tremendously rich, not only in its patristic roots, but also in the more recent developments of theology, for instance some aspects of Russian religious philosophy in the late nineteenth and early twentieth centuries. The undue monopoly of Schleiermacher on the one hand, and Hegel on the other, in contemporary Western theology, is based on one-sidedness and in part on ignorance. The Orthodox must speak out clearly of the God-centered anthropology of the Greek Fathers, and they will soon find influential allies in the West itself (for example much of Karl Rahner's work).

One should not forget, however, that by its very nature the true Christian message *cannot* be formulated in terms immediately understandable, and therefore appealing to the world. In becoming man and assuming the fullness of humanity the Son of God did not cater to any existing ideology or system of action. Neither can we. The Christian, for example, will necessarily be committed to social justice; but he will also have to warn that *ultimate* human destiny lies not simply in a just distribution of material goods. To those *believing* in social revolution he will necessarily appear as a rather shaky and uncommitted ally, reminding them that revolution is not the solution to all evils and that even it can become a true "opiate" of the people. With those on the right and those on the left the Christian can only go part of the way, and he is likely to disappoint both. His own total commitment will remain eschatological: "We look for the resurrection of the dead."

Thus the Church cannot identify itself totally with either social causes and ideologies of "change" or with the conservative philosophies of the *status quo*. However, there is a more natural and more reliable ally of Christianity which most Christians tend to overlook. This ally, I submit, is *science*.

The history of the relationship between Church and science is, as you know, a tragic one; and the Church is greatly responsible for the conflict. While the Western Church attempted to impose upon science its authoritarian control, which led to the development of antireligious "scientism" and positivism, the Orthodox East has often been too contemplative and (why hide it?) somehow monophysitic. It had little time to think of the problem. Modern science, moreover, was created in the European West and not in the Byzantine or Slavic East.

Nevertheless, today science and Christianity are no longer real enemies, but there is between them a tragic mutual ignorance. Christian theologians know little about science, partly because their own field is demanding enough, and partly because true science quickly discourages amateurs while sociology and politics do not, so that many theologians are tempted by easy and illusory success and become amateur sociologists and amateur politicians in order to be "in dialogue" with what they think is "the world." On the other hand, many scientists often know about Christianity no more than what they learned in their childhood on a grade school level. Meanwhile it is science and the technology streaming from it which control the contemporary world, rather than the politicians and social ideologists. The theologian and the scientist can and must understand each other. If they do not know each other, it is mostly because both have been conditioned by centuries of hostility, and because both were too busy with their respective parochial interests. Here is where the Church must manifest its *catholicity*, i.e. through overcoming all parochialism! Some of our contemporaries have shown the way: Paul Florensky in Russia, Teilhard de Chardin in the West. They may have made some intellectual mistakes, but shouldn't we forgive them when we think how tragically *alone* they were among the theologians of their time in their endeavor to show that theology and science are actually looking for the same and unique truth?

Here is where lies a most urgent "catholic" responsibility—not, of course, in the sense of promoting a new kind of "Orthodox science" which would know more about atoms, molecules, and genes than regular science, but in the sense of making theology and science consider each other seriously again. Today direct hostility between them has been largely overcome, but it has been replaced by mutual ignorance. The situation is that theologians recognize that science and technology represent a tremendous power for man, given by God to control nature. But scientists must also admit that their competence is limited by its very object. They establish facts, but the ultimate meaning of these facts escapes their domain. They should therefore look into *theology*, i.e. into the basic intellectual and spiritual implications of the faith for ultimate criteria and moral norms.


## Conclusion

These are some of the problems involved in our consideration of the catholicity of the Church. The real task lies ahead. Catholicity is not only to be discussed, but to be practiced. It is to be the obvious sign that each of our dioceses, each of our parishes, is indeed the local "catholic" Church, endowed with the divine gift of Christ's presence and called upon to manifest that gift to all men.

The great gap between theory and practice in the historical Orthodox Church of today would be grounds for despair among the Orthodox themselves, and for nothing but compassionate irony in those who look at us from out-

side, if theory were only "theory" and not a gift of God,
if the divine Eucharist were not transforming over and over
again our poor human fellowship into the true and catholic
Church of God, if, from time to time, God were not per-
forming miracles like permitting the survival of the Orthodox faith in oppressively secular societies or providing for
the Orthodox dispersion throughout the West, making possible a universal Orthodox witness again.

To close the gap and thus to become worthy of the
mighty acts of God so obviously performed for our benefit
and salvation, remains for us a sacred duty. The gap cannot
be closed through bluffing, lying, and boasting about the
past glories of this or that particular tradition, of this or
that ecclesiastical institution. There is one positive characteristic of the critical age in which we live: its ability to discern the unauthentic, its search for existential truth, its
search for holiness...

I have just used a word which indeed should not be
omitted in our discussion of catholicity. The Church is not
only one and catholic, it is also holy. Holiness is, of course,
a *divine* property, just like true oneness and true universality, but it is made accessible to man in the Church. Those
whom we call "saints" are precisely those Christians who,
more than others, have realized in themselves the fullness of
divine holiness communicated to men in the holy Church.
The Fathers of the Church, as we all know, never distinguished between "vision of God" and "theology." They
never admitted that intellectual prowess in understanding the
Gospel had any meaning without holiness. The saints—not
"professional churchmen"—have truly succeeded in projecting the image of Christ to the world in the past, for only
in the light of holiness can one truly understand the meaning of the cross and the meaning of St. Paul's description
of the Church in his own day: "We are treated as imposters,
and yet are true; as unknown, and yet well known; as dying,
and behold we live; as punished, and yet not killed; as sor-
rowful, yet always rejoicing; as poor, yet making many rich;
as having nothing, and yet possessing everything" (II Cor.
6:8-10).

# 6

# Contemporary Problems of Orthodox Canon Law*

If there is an area in which contemporary Orthodox thought can be said to be in crisis, it is certainly canon law. The crisis is obvious to ourselves and to the world around us. Conservatives and liberals, pro-ecumenists and anti-ecumenists, defenders of the *status quo* and reformers, are all invoking canons; but, in fact, no one seems to ask the fundamental question. What is the *nature* of the texts to which we are all referring? Are they all *legally* binding? Why, then, have some of them fallen into oblivion, without ever having been formally invalidated? If they are *not* legally binding, why do we invoke *some* of them so often? What is the criterion for making a selection? Is it not obvious that in our Orthodox Church, where there are so many divisions on practical issues and attitudes, each group finds canons seemingly justifying its own position, but forgets not only other texts, but more importantly, the *basic and consistent* Tradition of the Church? The latter is more important than particular canonical texts read out of their context. To discover what this basic Tradition is, is the essential task of theologians. It is because they too often ignore this task that there is in our midst the growing polarization between those who absolutize the *letter* of the canons (no one seems to absolutize *all* of them) and those who deny altogether

*Revised and augmented version of a paper originally published in *The Greek Orthodox Theological Review* vol. 17:1 (1972), pp. 41-50.

the validity of the Orthodox canonical corpus as it stands today. It is my conviction that both these groups are wrong.

On the official level of the various autocephalous churches the disturbing character of the situation has been recognized. The project of a new codification of canon law figures in all the schemes and programs prepared since the First World War in view of a forthcoming ecumenical, or "Great" Council of the Orthodox Church. Some preparation is going on even now, taking up the topics which we are discussing in this chapter. However, success in these endeavors is unlikely if a preliminary agreement is not reached concerning the *nature* of canon law.

## *I. Nature of Canon Law*

We are all familiar with St. Paul's attitude towards the Old Testament law: "Before the time for faith came, the Law kept us all locked as prisoners, until this coming faith should be revealed. So the Law was in charge of us, to be our *instructor* until Christ came, so that we might be put right with God through faith. Now that the time of faith is here, the *instructor* is no longer in charge of us" (Gal. 3:23-25). The difference between the situation which existed in the Old Testament and the "time of faith" in which we live, is that humanity does not need the mediation of an instructor (παιδαγωγός), that *salvation* is through faith, because if salvation were through the Law, Christ would have "died in vain."

With the coming of the Spirit salvation is a given experience, an immediate knowledge of God, a life "in Christ," experienced personally by each believer.

However, we all know that the New Testament in practically all its parts contains disciplinary and moral prescriptions which are seen as conditions for receiving and realizing salvation. The members of the Church of Christ are not fully realizing in themselves the life of the "New Adam" which is bestowed upon them in the sacraments. Somehow they still belong to the Old Adam also and, therefore, still

need a "pedagogue." They know, however, that legal prescriptions are not ends in themselves any more because salvation is "through faith." The law serves only as a means, adapted to concrete cases and concrete changing situations, for the
realization of true life in Christ. The "pedagogue" protects
the unchangeable content of salvation and goal of the faith
in the various and changing situations of history, which belong to life of the "Old Adam."

Following the pattern of the New Testament, the Church
has issued disciplinary rules and "canons" (actually "patterns") without which no visible organized society can exist
in the present *aion*. We ourselves, individually and collec-
tively, would be in great error if we believed that man could
reach the purely spiritual eschatological experience of the
Kingdom of God without the direction of a "pedagogue."
This "pedagogue"—whose function, I repeat, is not to provide salvation, but to delimit the conditions which make it
obtainable—is still with us in the form of the canons of
the Apostles, the Councils, and the Fathers. In turn these
are interpreted and applied in the particular disciplines of
particular churches, dioceses, and parishes.

During the Middle Ages when the Orthodox Church
lived in the tight framework of the Byzantine Empire, or
in the Orthodox empires of Bulgaria, Serbia and Russia,
practical necessity led to a codification of church canons
together with state legislation connected with religious
discipline. The results of these codifications are well known:
the various versions of the Byzantine *nomocanons* and the
Slavic *Kormchaya Kniga*, as well as several other codified
collections of canonical texts. No one would maintain that
these various codifications are adequate to the needs of the
Church today. While the ancient canons may remain as
criteria of church polity, the decrees of medieval emperors
have certainly lost their binding character. This fact was
already recognized in the eighteenth and the nineteenth centuries. The Greek Church adopted the so-called *Pedalion*, a
new compilation of canonical texts, as its standard manual.
The Church of Russia issued the so-called *Kniga Pravil*, a
collection of ancient canons (Apostles, Councils, Fathers),

together with commentaries by Aristenos, Zonaras and Balsamon. Both of these collections contain only ecclesiastical canons and no imperial decrees.

It can be said, therefore, that at no time in its history has the Orthodox Church ever had a *code* of canon law comparable to the *Corpus juris canonici* of the Roman Church. The medieval codes of the Christian East were both civil *and* ecclesiastical, while the new compilations (*Pedalion, Kniga Pravil*) are not "codes," but commented collections of ancient canons. In fact today each autocephalous Orthodox Church follows its own statute, which applies the principles found in the ancient canons to the concrete requirements of church life in specific parts of the world.

The problem faced by a new ecumenical council would consist first in answering the following questions. Is it possible or desirable to provide a standard codification of ancient canons which would be obligatory for the entire universal Orthodox Church? Since a codification would imply selection, what criteria should be used for such a selection?

Obviously, these criteria must be double.

(1)   Since, as we have seen above, the New Testamental justification of legal norms consists in their "pedagogical" value, those canons whose aim is to lead to a more perfect understanding of the eternal content of the Gospel and to protect the nature of the Church must be maintained and reaffirmed (cf. examples below).

(2)   Since the aim of the canons is to apply the content of the Christian faith to concrete situations, only those canons which can be directly or indirectly referred to the concrete situation *today* can retain validity; and certainly the Church must issue new practical directions in order to face new situations. As an example I can refer to the ancient canons concerned with the heretics and schismatics of the past. Contemporary heretics may be less or more dangerous to the Church, but they are not the same heretics as those of the past; and the possibility of a different canonical approach (more lenient, or more severe) must be at least envisaged, provided of course that it is fully consistent with the unchanging nature of the One Church.

The two criteria just mentioned cannot be defined with any degree of precision on purely *legal* grounds; they are *theological* criteria. Only theology—a biblical, traditional theology, fully consistent with the theology of the Councils and of the Fathers—can provide us with the necessary scale of values, by allowing us to discern the permanent truths which the ancient canonical texts are aiming to maintain.

The impossibility of applying purely *legal* categories can be illustrated by a number of cases where canons formally issued by ecumenical councils and never cancelled by anybody, are practically ignored (cf. Quinisext 14 on the age of ordination to the priesthood),[1] while others issued by local councils and by individual Fathers retain universal authority. The present confusion in our canonical thinking comes directly from constant misunderstanding of the true nature of the canonical tradition which expresses the Church's self-understanding in terms which cannot be *fully* reduced to legal categories. Those who try to affirm the legal absoluteness of all the canons are facing the fact that the Church has forgotten some of them for centuries. Those, on the contrary, who try to discount the entire tradition of the canons are actually dismissing the Church itself. The canonical fundamentalists and the liberals are *both* wrong in principle, in their very approach to the canons. The contemporary polarization between these two groups reflects an acute crisis of theology.

In interpreting each canonical text, or in issuing new ones, the Orthodox Church considers, in each case, first of all the Christian faith itself, and second the best way of preserving it today. It is according to this double criterion of *faith*, which must be preserved and proclaimed, that canons must be understood, eventually revised, and possibly renewed.

---

[1] Ordination of men below the age of thirty is considered as invalid, even if the candidate is "very worthy."

## II. Οἰκονομία *and* ἀκρίβεια

I have already mentioned the fact that in the Orthodox
Church the basis of canon law is not a fixed "code" but a
collection of ancient texts issued under circumstances quite
different from ours, but valid inasmuch as they reflect the
doctrinal *content* of the Christian faith, or its implications.
This situation gives a particular importance to what we call
*economy* (οἰκονομία), a concept quite current in patristic
thought to designate *God's plan for the salvation of man*.
It is precisely in this soteriological context that St. Basil has
defined the canonical concept of "economy" in his famous
letter to Amphilochius. He allows the recognition of the
Novatian baptism in order to avoid putting "an obstacle to
the general plan of salvation" (οἰκονομία τῶν πολλῶν).[2]
Quite mistakenly, in my opinion, the concept of *economy*
is sometimes given the narrow legal sense of "dispensation,"
and thus opposed to "exactness" (ἀκρίβεια). This use of
the term is correct in some instances, when "economy," i.e.
the concern for man's salvation requires actions contrary to
the *letter* of the law; but there are also cases when economy,
i.e. concern for man's salvation, requires absolute strictness
(even beyond the letter). Examples occurred when the
Church decided to practice rebaptism of Western Christians
in the seventeenth century, or more recently when the validity
of apostolic succession was denied to bishops and priests
who received orders in the "Renovated" church in Russia.
On the other hand, economy can be a part of the canon itself,
as for example in canon 8 of Nicaea, which admits that
Novatian bishops coming to the Church should be recognized
as bishops whenever the Church needs bishops, and as priests
when such need does not exist.

"Economy," therefore, is not an *arbitrary* concept. One
cannot, for example, recognize "by economy" the baptism
of somebody who was never baptized (a non-Christian for
example). But positive recognition is determined by the good
of the Church. When the Church recognizes *by economy*

[2]St. Basil, *Letter* 188, ed. R. J. Deferrari (Loeb Classical Library), vol. 3,
p. 18.

the sacraments performed outside of the Orthodox Church, it certainly does not give existence "by economy" to something which did not exist previously, but it *discerns* the reality of sacramental grace bestowed outside the normal canonical boundaries of the Church. The practice of such a *discernment* is an act of "economy," i.e. of concern for the salvation of all. It is a recognition that God continues to work for the salvation of mankind, sometimes by means which do not conform to the canons. It is not only the right but also the duty of the Church to recognize such a divine action, just as it is also its duty to deny the very possibility of divine grace in groups whose aim is to destroy the Church of God, or to interrupt its Spirit-guided Tradition.

### III. New canonical legislation is desirable

There are several areas where new canonical and disciplinary definitions would help the Orthodox Church to face the contemporary world. One question, however, requires action more urgently than any other, the local or "territorial" principle of church life and administration. There cannot exist any doctrinal, disciplinary, missionary, or canonical justification for the state of canonical chaos in which the Orthodox Church lives, for example, in America. The situation is made more dramatic by the fact that no one—not even the sister churches, the bishops, the theologians, not to speak of the average priest or layman—seems to recognize that the revealed God-established *norm* of church unity is being forgotten and, in fact, consciously rejected, when one admits as normal the existence of several "jurisdictions" side by side in the same place. I have discussed elsewhere the ecclesiological, canonical and practical issues involved in this question,[3] and others have done it even better. It is obvious that the formal rejection of the territorial norm, the concept that each Orthodox autocephalous or national church has *de jure* a universal jurisdiction over all members of a particular

[3] *Orthodoxy and Catholicity* (New York: Sheed and Ward, 1966), pp. 107-118.

ethnic group wherever they are found (i.e. the Church of Russia over all the Russians, the Church of Constantinople over all the Greeks, etc.) is not only unpractical, because it is often impossible to define ethnicity, but also formally racist and, in fact, heretical. Christ came to establish on earth a new and holy nation, a *tertium genus*, a kingdom which is "not of this world." A church whose only function is to maintain ethnic identification loses the character of true "Church of God." It is unable to fulfill its mission, for it is formally exclusive of those who do not belong to its ethnicity. To maintain, as is often done, that our ethnic divisions do not prevent us from being in eucharistic communion with each other, and that therefore we keep "spiritual" unity, is obviously insufficient (and often hypocritical) because in Orthodox ecclesiology the Eucharist is the *pattern* of church life and structure. If we celebrate the Eucharist without following the pattern it implies—"one church, one bishop in each place"—we are in fact betraying its meaning, and probably even partake of the Body and Blood of Christ "for our condemnation."

The territorial principle was universally applied in the Orthodox Church until it was formally broken for the first time in America in 1921. In 1872, the Council of Constantinople condemned the Bulgarians for the heresy of "phyletism," which consisted precisely in promoting the ethnic principle in church administration. Obviously, the responsibilities in the Greco-Bulgarian struggle of the last century were at least mutual, but the *formal* decision of the council, rejecting as "phyletistic" the project which would have accepted the parallel existence on the same territory of two churches, the Greek and the Bulgarian, was formally quite legitimate and accepted as such by all the autocephalous churches. It is really frightening to think how far we have gone since that time in America. Is it not assumed as self-evident that there are now in America the "Greek Church," the "Ukrainian Church," the "Serbian Church"? We have exactly the situation which St. Paul condemns, which the entire Holy Tradition ignores and which was formally condemned by the Patriarchate of Constantinople in 1872.

Of course there is no question that the national traditions of the various Orthodox peoples are closely knit together with the Church. It is the Church which has traditionally maintained their cultural identity. The strength of this tradition is not negative in itself; the so-called "Cyrillo-Methodian" heritage, allowing and promoting the use of the vernacular in the liturgy and the subsequent growth of national Orthodox cultures in the Slavic countries must and can be preserved. The unprecedented massive immigration of various ethnic groups to America, the peculiar social laws followed by these immigrants, the open character of American society which encourages the preservation of ethnic identities, are all to be taken into consideration. Why can't the various national heritages be preserved in a united Church? Are the Irish, the Polish, the Italian, and the other identities dissolved in a united Roman Catholicism? A canonically united Orthodox Church can indeed provide all the necessary guarantees, respecting wherever necessary the peculiarities and identities of everyone on the diocesan or parish levels. But the Church must manifest its visible God-established unity. It must be seen as Kingdom of God, as a missionary community, open to all and transcending (not suppressing) all human cultural values. For these values, if they are not transcended, become idols and are, as such, abominations in the eyes of God.

Practically, we would need a new canon officially sanctioned by an ecumenical council, which would proclaim and require the following: "In areas and countries where two or more Orthodox autocephalous churches are sending clergy to exercise a permanent ministry, canonical order requires the establishment of a united Church. Procedures to be followed are to be elaborated by consultation between all parties involved on the universal or local level. Pluralism of languages and traditions will be maintained and guaranteed wherever necessary, through the establishment of appropriate structures organized on a temporary basis."

*IV. Possible revision of existing canonical legislation*

The so-called "Renovated" schism in Russia (1922-1944) initiated a series of radical canonical reforms, which obviously did not belong to the competence of one single local church and which were undertaken without any serious concern for the basic tenets of Holy Tradition. The failure and condemnation of the "Renovated" Church compromised, in the eyes of many, the very idea of canonical reform. Actually, this was not the first time in history that a sectarian movement provoked a conservative reaction which rejected even the good aspects of proposed reform, only because the latter had been proposed by schismatics.

The "Renovated" Church, as was clearly shown by Professor S. V. Troitsky,[4] was a revolt led by married priests fighting for their "rights" against a "despotic" celibate episcopate and sceptic laity. The "professional" claims of the "Renovated" clergy included the restoration of a married episcopate and the permission to clerics to marry—even a second time—after ordination.

The "Renovated" schism is now dead, but it is well-known that some of the questions it raised were not clearly answered by the church actions condemning the schismatics. In many Orthodox circles the question of the relation between ordination and marriage are openly debated, and "liberal" as well as "conservative" statements on the question are made by hierarchs and theologians. However, the full range of issues implied is very rarely seen or acknowledged. I am deliberately choosing this issue for discussion as a test case, with the understanding that canonical revisions are possible in other areas as well, provided one keeps in mind the basic presuppositions related to the faith itself.

We have accepted the principle that disciplinary canons are changeable in every aspect which does not involve the substance of the faith. This is the very basis of the principle of *oikonomia*, as defined by St. Basil and Patriarch Photius.

[4]The original Russian text of S. V. Troitsky's book was translated into English in W. C. Emhardt, *Religion in Soviet Russia* (London: Mowbrays, 1929).

How does this principle apply to the three issues under consideration, which are:

(1) election of married men to the episcopate.

(2) marriage after ordination.

(3) admission to the clergy of men who had married more than once, or whose wife was married previously, and permission for widowed priests to marry again?

In the first case the ancient church Tradition, which knew married bishops, is eloquent enough. No doctrinal issue is involved and a new ecumenical council can change the canon (Sixth Ecumenical Council, 48) which requires that candidates for the episcopate either be celibates or be separated from their wives at their consecration. The only warning which can be issued against such a reform is that it would provide no guarantee that the best candidates would actually be chosen for the episcopate anyway.

In dealing with the second and the third issues it is first of all necessary to see that they involve clearly distinct problems. There is first the problem of marriage after ordination. There does not seem to be any theological issue involved in bestowing this sacrament upon men who are already in the holy orders. But the canonical legislation which forbids this practice (Apostolic Canon 26; Sixth Ecumenical Council, 6, etc.) is based on serious pastoral and practical considerations. A priest should be a mature man, having reached full life stability; and what is less stable than a man looking for a wife? What would parishioners think if their pastor and "father in Christ" would look for a bride in their midst? This pastoral aspect of the problems does carry much weight and I personally do not think that changing the present canonical requirements is really desirable.

But the issue is much more serious in the third case. There doctrine—New Testament doctrine on marriage—is clearly involved. Not only is there the clear requirement of I Tim. 3:2, 12 and Tit. 1:6, but it is unavoidable to remember that second marriage is admitted by the Church exclusively as a toleration, never as a norm. The New Testament norm of marriage is a unique and eternal bond between two beings, in the image of God and Israel, of Christ and the Church (Eph. 5). Until the tenth century second marriages were never blessed in Church and required a long period of penance.[5] For laymen, such marriages are admitted "by economy," as a lesser evil (I Cor. 7:8-9) or as a new chance to build up a life. How could priests preach *such* a doctrine of marriage, if they themselves did not practice it? The canonical legislation forbidding men married twice to be ordained, or priests to remarry protect not only priesthood, but also the Church's doctrine on marriage.

We all know that this legislation may provoke personal tragedies, especially in the cases of young priests with children who lose their wives. But, were not such tragedies even more frequent in the past, with a higher mortality rate among young women? Did they prevent the Church from maintaining its doctrine on marriage, based on an eschatological interpretation of the bond of love, which is not broken by death? Could not some aspects of the tragedy (care for children) be moderated by the Church, so that the sanctity of marriage may be preserved at least in the person of the priests?

## V. Primacy of Constantinople and the Autocephalous Churches

There is no controversy in the Orthodox Church concerning the origin and the nature of the "primacy of honor" and the "privileges" (πρεσβεῖα) of the "ecumenical patriarch" of Constantinople. Early Christian and contemporary Orthodox ecclesiology excludes the idea of a primacy "by divine right." It does allow and even require, however, a certain "order" between the local churches, which is necessitated by the conditions of the life of the Church in the present *aion*. If the witness and action of the One Church is to remain truly united, it must also be orderly. Constantinople occupies the first rank in that "order" because Rome,

---

[5]Cf. a more developed treatment of the issue in my book on *Marriage: An Orthodox Perspective* (Crestwood, N. Y.: St. Vladimir's Seminary Press, second edition, 1974).

the previous "No. 1," broke its communion with the Orthodox patriarchal sees and, therefore, lost its primatial position among them.

The position of "second in rank" has been granted to
Constantinople not for any theological reason, but for a
purely pragmatic one; it was the new capital of the Empire.[6] Although the political reason which motivated the
canons recognizing that position of Constantinople has now
disappeared, there remains a consensus in the Orthodox
Church to maintain their validity even under present historical conditions. The conservative instinct of the Church
acts in favor of this consensus, and also there is clearly an
advantage in having the primate reside in a country whose
government is not directly involved in Orthodox affairs. In
fact, contemporary Constantinople's (or Istanbul's) primacy
can be justified by arguments opposite to those which originally created it. There is *no* Orthodox emperor in Istanbul,
and this is why Constantinople's bishop could exercise a useful and fully independent ministry of coordination and
arbitration, if he were given the means of doing so.

The actual rights of the patriarch of Constantinople are
the normal consequence and expression of his being the
"first" among Orthodox bishops: chairmanship at Pan-
Orthodox meetings and a certain responsibility (although
not a monopoly) for initiating common action. In addition,
canons 9 and 17 of the Fourth Ecumenical Council of Chalcedon grant him the right to receive appeals against the
judgment of local provincial synods. Before the fall of Constantinople (1453) the patriarch of Constantinople did exercise *de facto* a much larger power and influence over the
entire Orthodox world.[7] After 1453, in the framework of
the Ottoman imperial administration of the Balkans and the

---

[6]Cf. canon 3 of Constantinople II (381) and canon 28 of Chalcedon
(451).

[7]On the historical background of this extraordinary position of Constantinople in the Middle Ages see our two articles "Society and Culture in the
Fourteenth Century: Religious Problems," *Actes du XIVe Congrès International
des Etudes Byzantines* I (Bucharest, 1974), pp. 111-124; and "Byzantium
from 1071 to 1261: Ideological Crises," *Actes du XVe Congrès International
des Etudes Byzantines* (Athens, 1976).

entire Middle East, he received additional political responsibilities for the entire Orthodox population of the Turkish
empire.[8]

These uncontroversial historical facts are necessary for
the understanding of the present situation, in which the actual
role of the ecumenical patriarch of Constantinople in universal Orthodoxy has, indeed, become a matter of debate.[9]
Again, the controversy is not about the origin or the very
existence of the primacy, but about its practical application
five centuries after the fall of Byzantium and one century
after the end of the Ottoman rule in the Balkans and the
Middle East. The debate simply cannot be brought to a
fruitful conclusion unless everyone acknowledges the rather
obvious fact that both the Byzantine and the Ottoman empires do not exist anymore, and that the world to which
Orthodox witness is to be made relevant is a world dominated
by other powers and realities.

The reality which is particularly harmful to Orthodox
witness in the present world, and also to the true manifesta-
tion of Orthodox ecclesiology, has been mentioned above.
It is *ethnic nationalism* (as distinct from sound and legitimate cultural patriotism), inherited from the nineteenth
century. Because of this, contemporary Orthodoxy looks like
a loose federation of ethnic churches, frequently quarreling
with each other, rather than the One Catholic Church of
Christ. Doctrinally this ethnic nationalism has been officially
condemned by the Orthodox Church of Constantinople in
1872, but it still dominates in practice much of the relations
between the Orthodox autocephalous churches. In America,
for example, it is even accepted as the only practical principle of church organization, so that the establishment of an
"Orthodox Church in America" which is neither Greek, nor
Russian, nor Arab, but welcomes all, including plain Americans, has created quite a storm of opposition.

[8]On this period, see S. Runciman, *The Great Church in Captivity* (Cambridge, 1968).

[9]See, for example, the correspondence between the patriarchates of Constantinople and Moscow concerning the American autocephaly: the complete
text of all the documents is available in an English translation in *St.
Vladimir's Theological Quarterly* vol. 15 (1971).

These are the realities which demand a new, direct and clear canonical legislation, if—as all Orthodox admit—canons are intended to spell out the practical requirements of Orthodox doctrine. If there is an aspect of the existing canons which can be preserved and reaffirmed, it is precisely the primacy of a supra-national center capable of acting as an arbiter and a convener, responsible for Orthodox unity and order, and independent from the various particular ethnic interests represented by the various national autocephalous churches.

We would rather not return to the sad conditions which have recently prevented Constantinople from playing this role, particularly in connection with the American situation. On the contrary, we would suggest that Constantinople, in virtue of its acknowledged primacy, be made responsible for enforcing the new and unambiguous canonical legislation which we have suggested above in paragraph 3 of this chapter, by organizing, sponsoring, and guiding the necessary consultations between the autocephalous churches. Similar consultations, leading to joint decisions, would of course also be necessary in order to insure a unified Orthodox attitude in ecumenical, social, and missionary matters. In order to be successful, the ecumenical patriarchate would probably have to be organized into a truly international center, with all the churches appointing members to its staff (cf. our observations above, p. 89.)

Such clear responsibilities—formally defined and excluding all power *over* the local churches—would make the ecumenical patriarchate (even it it is obliged one day to leave Turkish Istanbul, where the conditions necessary for its international activity do not exist) a true center of Orthodox conciliarity. It is indeed refreshing that a recent book on the ecumenical patriarchate by Metropolitan Maximos of Sardis defines the primacy of Constantinople in terms of *service* (διακονία) to all the churches. This is, indeed, the theological and ecclesiological category which makes the idea of primacy acceptable and ancient canons fully understandable, while remaining fully adequate to the new historical situation in which we live. The ecumenical patriarch cannot make his primacy relevant simply by trying to impress upon the contemporary Orthodox churches that the "barbarian lands," mentioned in canon 28 of Chalcedon, and for which the patriarchate of Constantinople was supposed to appoint bishops in Byzantine times, actually mean Western Europe, America, or Japan. His role rather consists in assuming moral and canonical leadership and affirming unquestionable principles of Orthodox ecclesiology, particularly the unity of all the Orthodox living in one geographic area, and common witness to the non-Orthodox and the non-Christian world.

These are the questions which will have to be debated at the proposed Orthodox ecumenical council, if the question is raised at its sessions of new canonical legislation on these issues. Neither cheap liberalism, nor superficial modernism, nor blind canonical fundamentalism will then help the Fathers of the Council to remain like their predecessors the living instruments of the Holy Spirit. Certainly the Spirit of the Gospel, as well as an enlightened theological faithfulness to Holy Tradition, will be the only acceptable criteria in the revision of age-old canonical rules.

# 7

# Confessing Christ Today*

One of the cardinal principles of Christian life is that closeness to Christ brings about also the closeness of Christians to each other. This closeness, however, necessarily involves tension and even tragedy, because in this world there are powers resisting Christ. Thus not only does the Christian message itself lead, in fact, to division ("I came not to send peace, but a sword," Matt. 10:34), but controversy even surrounded Jesus during his lifetime. His own physical presence had no magically unifying effect; and His doctrine, or doctrines about Him, do not bring automatic unanimity. When He taught, there was constant conflict even among the "religious people" of His day. He was even the object of their "hatred" and predicted the same to His disciples, because "the servant is not greater than his master" (John 15:20). The history of the Church is full of doctrinal struggles about Christ's identity and the meaning of His work. All sides in these struggles claimed to be "close" to Him and to express His teaching adequately.

In what sense then is it possible to say, as we do, that the unity of the Church is *in Christ?* For clearly our Christian faith does not allow us to look for any other form of unity or any other pattern that would make the Church *one.* Indeed "unity" in Christ is mysterious in nature. It does not follow an exclusively intellectual pattern. It is not limited to

*A paper delivered on June 5, 1974, at the monastery of Cernica, Romania, during a consultation of Orthodox theologians on "Confessing Christ Today," and published originally in *St. Vladimir's Theological Quarterly* vol. 18:4 (1974), pp. 156-65.

a unity of conviction, nor is it simply emotional faithfulness
to a beloved Master. Even if it includes and presupposes these
patterns, it is certainly not exhausted by them. What then
is its nature?

## *I. Unity in Christ*

Orthodox theology understands "unity in Christ" as a
*communion* in the risen and ascended Body of the New Man.
"You are dead," writes St. Paul, "and your life is hidden
in God with Christ" (Col. 3:3). There is, therefore, a particular manner in which we achieve this closeness to Christ
which makes the Church to be one. This manner, which
Paul calls "communion," transcends intellectual conviction,
moral commitment or ethical principle. It is indicated by
several major biblical and patristic themes. In Isaiah we find
the mysterious image of the *Suffering Servant* which is applicable both to the collective reality of Israel, the people of
God, and to the unique person of Jesus. In the Pauline doctrines of Jesus as the *New Adam* and of the Church as *Body
of Christ*, the community is again assumed by this unique
person. The theme of *recapitulation*, made prominent by
St. Irenaeus, implies that generations of mankind and centuries of history found their center and ultimate meaning in
Christ. According to St. Gregory of Nyssa's concept *the
image of God* in man belongs not so much to human individuals taken separately, as to mankind as a whole, re-
capitulated in its model, Christ.

All these themes are also presupposed in the Orthodox
Chalcedonian and post-Chalcedonian Christology, which affirms that in Christ, the divine hypostasis of the pre-existing
and eternal Logos, one of the Holy Trinity, assumed not only
an individual man but also the whole of human nature.
Thus, in unity with Christ and in Christ, we enter into real
communion not only with God Himself, but also with each
other and with the entire communion of saints past and present. In other words, we become members of the One, Holy,
and Catholic Church. Indeed, the unity, the holiness, and

the catholicity of the Church are *in Christ.* But they are "hidden in God with Christ." Even in the greatest among the saints, they appear only partially—not to speak of the vast majority of us, who call ourselves Christians but who in fact live "according to the elements of this world." The risen Lord and His power of immortality remain "hidden" to the eyes of the world.

This "hiddenness" of the Church's true nature does not mean that it is only a "celestial" reality in a Platonic sense. On earth, in the midst of the inevitable pluralism of the historical process, where not only God but also Satan is claiming the allegiance of man, the Church does maintain a stability and a continuity. These are best expressed in the fourth *nota ecclesiae,* her apostolicity, i.e. her connection with and dependence upon the "witnesses of the Resurrection" and the Christ-selected heralds of the original Christian Gospel.

However, formal apostolicity is only a condition for unity in Christ, not its very content. The content is "life in Christ," a communion with God. This communion always implies cooperation (or "synergy") between the divine gift and human free acceptance and effort. Such cooperation was fully achieved in the hypostatic union between the divine and the human wills of Jesus Christ; and we also are able to strive for it, because from the ascended Christ we have received the "other Comforter," the Spirit of Christ, through whom the hidden divine life is made accessible to mankind.

Thus through the Spirit, the oneness of Christ, as the unique Savior, the unique God, becomes also oneness for the Church without suppressing the diversity, the freedom, the personal variety of God's creation. This is beautifully expressed in the hymnography of Pentecost.

> The Spirit bestows all things; it appoints prophets; it consecrates priests; it gives wisdom to the simple; it turned fishermen into theologians; it gathers together the whole assembly of the Church. O Comforter, consubstantial and co-reigning with the Father and the Son, glory to Thee!

We have seen the true light; we have received the
heavenly Spirit; we have found the true faith, worshipping the undivided Trinity, who has saved us!

Pentecost is an eschatological feast, and the Book of
Acts testifies to the fulfillment on that day of the Messianic
prophecy of Joel (Acts 2:16ff; Joel 3:1-5). In a very direct sense, communion in the oneness of Christ is, each time,
the renewal of Pentecost. Therefore the most perfect form
of communion, the moment when the Kingdom of God becomes truly accessible to man, the time when the Church *is*
most truly the Body of Christ, occurs through an invocation
of the Spirit, a calling upon Him to come "upon us and upon
these gifts" (eucharistic canon). Then, in spite of our sins
and deficiencies, we, as the community, become the Church
of God and commune in the unity of Christ through the
mystery of the Eucharist. This is, in fact, the goal of our existence as Christians, the "perfection of life in Christ"
(Nicholas Cabasilas, *Life in Christ*, IV, 1), "the mystery
which supplies perfection to the other mysteries" (*ibid*. IV,
3) and makes the church to be the Church. It is around
and because of the Eucharist that the Church is organized
the way it is: eucharistic unity in each place, pastoral duties
and preaching performed by the one who also performs the
Eucharist, identity of all local churches in the face of God,
full "catholicity" of each of them as the "catholic church"
in each place (Ignatius of Antioch, *Smyr.* 8:2).

This eucharistic unity in Christ does not produce any
magical transformation of sinful human beings. It leaves
intact human freedom and responsibility. However, it does
allow man to partake of the resurrected and victorious
Christ, anticipating the time when Christ will be "all in all"
and when the absoluteness of His power will become manifest
in the ultimate eschatological fulfillment. Until that time
the gift of communion with Christ—that which the Fathers
also call "deification"—remains hidden under sacramental
veils and requires from every one of us the ascetical struggle,
the struggle against the passions, the efforts of the will, and
"synergy" between divine grace and the imperfect possibilities

of fallen human nature. Its concrete realization in the structures and conditions of the fallen cosmos can only be partial,
even if it allows each one of us to participate in the immortality of the risen Lord, even in this life where death still
reigns. The saints are witness of this fact.

## II. *"Today"*

I do not think that many among Orthodox theologians
will object to the substance of what I have stated above;
this is, indeed, the basic content of the Orthodox understanding of salvation and, as such, it is not controversial. The
problem arises with the adverb "today." What are the difficulties which arise when we speak about Christ in such
terms and about the Church, as "one in Christ" in the contemporary ecumenical or secular context?

It is clear, for example, that the past decade, a time when
practically all Orthodox churches had joined the World
Council of Churches, was also a period of theological
polarization; and, in fact, many Orthodox felt that there
was an increasing gap between the dominant concerns of the
Council and the basic Orthodox understanding of salvation
in Christ. This estrangement, which is recognized today even
by the highest authorities in Orthodoxy, was not due to a
weakening in the *content* of the Orthodox witness. If one
reads objectively the contributions made by individual Orthodox participants in the various assemblies, conferences, and
consultations during that period, one will find—in spite of
differences of emphasis, which always have existed between
the more "liberal" and the more "conservative" traditions in
Orthodox theology—the same basic faithfulness to the Orthodox idea of "communion in Christ," of deification, of the
sacraments understood in their ecclesiological context, etc.
The unenlightened and fanatical criticism in some ultra-
conservative Orthodox circles of the contemporary Orthodox
participation in the ecumenical movement, as being a sell-
out to Protestantism, has no real foundation.

Nevertheless, for whatever reason, the impact of Orthodoxy on the overall work of the Council has been quite insufficient, with the possible exception of some individual "Faith and Order" studies. It is our duty, as Orthodox theologians, to ask the question: Why?

In this perspective I wish to point out two major and connected factors, both of which obviously have contributed to the relative insufficiency of the Orthodox ecumenical witness to the unity of the Church, insufficiency not in content but in *persuasiveness*. Though the Orthodox truth is in itself unchangeable, its verbal expressions and practical applications may certainly change; and thus it is still fully legitimate to ask for a convincing and contemporary Orthodox witness in the context of today's ecumenical movement.

(1) Although the Orthodox Church consistently claims to be the One Church, and thus to possess the unity already given in Christ, it hardly presents to the outside world *a public image* confirming that claim. Its divisions are there to see, and I would even say that they appear more serious to the outside observer than to the Orthodox themselves. For we Orthodox do indeed find the way, sometimes almost unconsciously, to experience our unity in faith which transcends all empirical divisiveness. We experience it in the liturgical mystery as well as in our real fellowship of mind and thought. But outside observers, including our colleagues and fellow-ecumenists, are not personally initiated into the mysteries of this fellowship. They can only observe our obvious inability to translate our unity in faith into unity in life and action, and they cannot seriously be blamed for the unfavorable conclusion which they draw from our state of paralysis.

One should keep in mind also that the divisions in contemporary Orthodoxy are not divisions only in ecumenical tactics, manifested in our obvious unpreparedness and lack of coordination in the sphere of ecumenical relations. One can even say that the commendable efforts and achievements of recent Pan-Orthodox conferences and consultations have begun to alleviate the crisis in this respect. What is more serious, in my opinion, is not our lack of monolithic unity in our witness *ad extra*, but the *de facto* acceptance by us Ortho-

dox of secular divisiveness in the very structure of our own
church life. Let us consider the most obvious example.

One of the characteristics of Christian expansion in Eastern Europe has been the adoption by the Orthodox Church
of ethnic characteristics, its rapid "indigenization." Here lies
its unquestionable strength, its contribution to the creation
of national cultures, but also a temptation which today has
become a veritable disease. The Church quite legitimately
can find in national cultures a vehicle for the promotion of
the Christian faith. But is it legitimate to let the nations use
the Church in their own interests? It is not my intention
here to pass judgement on all individual cases, on particular
tragedies and difficulties, for they all point to a *general*
phenomenon which prevents many of us even from seeing
the problem. The most obvious and the worst case is the
situation of the Orthodox Church in Western countries.
There, with the formal consent of almost all of our local
churches, the system branded as "phyletistic heresy" by the
Synod of Constantinople of 1872[1] is accepted as the *de facto*
*norm* for the organization of Church. This fact is not only
of practical, administrative importance. It is indeed also a
theological and doctrinal issue: an issue about the *nature* of
Church unity.

It is sometimes said that administrative disunity is admissible, since we have unity in faith and sacraments. To say
this is exactly the same as to say that faith and sacraments
are only "spiritual" reality, which do not obligate us to any
real and concrete common life. It is an implicit acceptance
of a *docetic* Christology, fought against by St. Ignatius of
Antioch in the first century. As Jews and Greeks were refusing to form one church and wanted to form two separate
communities in Corinth, Paul did not tell them: "This is admissible, since you are anyway spiritually one." He asked,
"Is Christ divided?"

My first point is that it is difficult to maintain a truly

---

[1]"Phyletism," defined and condemned as heresy by the Synod of Constantinople in 1872, with the participation of other Eastern Patriarchs, is the
acceptance of purely ethnic norms in the administration of the Church. In
practice, it involved the creation of two distinct churches, the Greek and the
Bulgarian, on the same territory in the southern Balkans.

*Christological* criterion for Church unity in ecumenical debates when one does not accept this criterion for oneself. Have not we ourselves reduced our "unity in Christ" to a spiritual abstraction by implicitly but quite practically surrendering to secularism in adopting secular, ethnic, and political criteria to shape our concrete existence as a Christian community?

(2)   My second point refers to the general tendency to intepret the Christian witness of salvation and liberation in socio-political terms. It seems to me that if we are to present a distinct and relevant Orthodox contribution to the debate, we have to learn the methodology of a *critical* dialogue in the framework of the ecumenical movement. Simple doctrinal statements on the nature of the saving Christian faith, as understood by the Orthodox, are clearly insufficient for doing justice to the problem. We have to learn to understand others and to criticize them with understanding. In that respect, we are witnessing the beginning of responsible criticism of some major trends in the World Council. An impressive convergnce of position is appearing. I am thinking, of course, of the statements made in Geneva on behalf of the patriarchates of Constantinople and Moscow. A long encyclical letter "On Christian Unity," published by the bishops of the Orthodox Church in America, also has found a widespread response. This convergence of Orthodox witness, clearly unplanned and spontaneous, needs to be pushed further in the form of a precise theological challenge whose aim would be not the end of the ecumenical movement but its revival as a living dialogue.

Here are some theological affirmations which, in my opinion, constitute the essential Orthodox witness in the ecumenical movement:

[a] *Authentic human life presupposes not a secular "unity of mankind" but communion with God.* This affirmation is based on the doctrine of the "image of God" in man, but also on Christology. Jesus is the perfect man, *not in spite of* His being also perfect God, but *because* He is also God. One can say that, historically, one of the most lasting misunderstandings between East and West has been related

to anthropology. There is an inherent trend in Western theology towards defining man as an *autonomous* being, and it is against the background of this autonomy that man is declared "guilty" of sin or "justified" or "saved." This Western trend is clearly sympathetic to a Nestorianizing Christology which would affirm the divinity and the humanity of Christ but would describe their union as a juxtaposition, excluding all "communication of idioms." Contemporary theological scholarship, based on these presuppositions, interprets the Greek patristic ideas of "communion" and "deification" as Neoplatonic deviation. This contemporary "secularism" in theology is the extreme point of a developing trend which is only occasionally balanced by other tendencies in contemporary Western thought (for example the "theocentric anthropology" of Karl Rahner).

It is therefore our duty as Orthodox to challenge the "secular" idea of man. The practical implications are obvious, especially in the field of ethics. Christians cannot be Christians without being concerned with feeding the hungry and liberating the oppressed; but, once fed and liberated, the hungry and the oppressed may still be devoid of communion with eternal life. The better fed societies are frequently the most corrupt! It is *eternal life*—the true destiny of man in Christ—which Christianity is all about. Compared with it, social progress is a *relative* though authentic value, sometimes better served and achieved by non-Christians. We can certainly *assume* this progress and label it as an expression of the same Logos, but it will always lack completeness without Christ.

[b] *Christian Faith implies free conversion and sanctification of the person*, and is not an ideological tool for the betterment of the "fallen" world. "Communion" and "deification" are always an interpersonal process between the Living God and man. Only a person can be baptized, not an institution, a social theory, or a philosophical ideology. Only a person can ultimately be "saved" and "redeemed"; and salvation always implies an interplay between the divine all-powerful gift of grace and man's free response, and never the magical sanctification of a thing or an idea. Matter is

indeed sanctified in the Eucharist, but as the "Bread of Heaven" which is offered to *man* so that he might partake of it. Only living and personal beings can be truly *thankful*, i.e. truly participate in the Eucharist. Similarly, the Church represents a unity in Christ of living free persons, gathered together by the power of the Holy Spirit. It is not an impersonal institution established *over* them.

This initial and fundamental personalism of the Christian faith, and therefore also of ecclesiology and of soteriology, is understood one-sidedly by Protestant "fundamentalists" when they reduce Christianity to a personal *emotional experience.* Thus they frequently preach that Christianity should "stay out of politics" in a way that in fact implies uncritical acceptance of the social and political *status quo.* Similarly, in the Orthodox East, an artificial separation between the "spiritual" and the "material" leads at times to the same practical conclusions. However, the Orthodox Christian belief in the Incarnation of the Logos recognizes in Him not only a subjective truth, or the object of an emotional experience, but also the total and cosmic Truth, the meaning and the reason of all things even before the Incarnation. This belief is, of course, the theology of Colossians; and it culminates in the patristic tradition with St. Maximus the Confessor. It makes, for the Christian faith, a universal "catholic" claim. It excludes all Manicheism or absenteeism. Nothing created by God is evil in itself, and all creation is a living concern to the Christian. This Christian faith also reveals to the Christian who acquires the divine *gnosis* of the fullness of truth in Christ how different the *fallen* world is from God's design, how strong are the disruptive forces of evil, how unique and irreplaceable is the *hidden mystery* of the Spirit for the knowledge of the full meaning of things. Because he knows the access to the one source of the true meaning for the whole of creation, the Christian will seek, first of all, to get closer to that source, and will certainly not be tempted to accept uncritically solutions coming from other sources. He will be anything but a "secularist."

[c] *Christ alone, through the Holy Spirit, gives authenticity to any form of true Church unity.* This affirmation

stands very much in the center of the ecumenical dialogue in all its aspects, but it acquires a very particular significance if one stands by the principles of Orthodox Christology. If the real new life of the risen Lord is indeed accessible to man, no substitute for it is possible at all. On this point the discussion in the fourteenth century between Barlaam the Calabrian and St. Gregory Palamas is of great interest today. It was concerned with the questions of whether knowledge of God and communion with God are really a *givenness*, or whether they are only philosophical conjectures. Similarly, Church unity can be seen either as already *given*, or as a goal proposed to human efforts and, therefore, inaccessible in its fullness. Clearly, Orthodox Christology requires the first alternative. However, it also knows the tension between the *already given* and *not yet*. This opposition is not an artificial opposition between the institution and the event. It, in fact, coincides with the Pauline opposition between the "old" and the "new" Adam. It exists in each person, in the struggle of each one of us with passion and sin. Can the Church be truly *one* in terms of the "old" Adam? Can there be *sin* in that *oneness*? Are not separation, divisiveness, and conflict inevitable wherever the "Divider" (διάβολος) still possesses his power? Do not the concepts of unity, love, and reconciliation have only a *relative* meaning in the fallen world? But, *not in Christ*.

Thus, when we Orthodox insist that only a true confession of Christ, in the fullness of His given Truth, in the fullness of sacramental communion, are adequate expressions of the unity of the Church, we are simply maintaining the only realistic and acceptable goal of the ecumenical movement. The recent over-involvement of the World Council in that which was called the "horizontal concerns" is wrong, not simply because it represents a return to "Life and Work" away from "Faith and Order" (the opposition is theologically artificial), but also because it is frequently by definition *divisive*. The present World Council membership can speak in a united voice only when and if it speaks in Christian terms. Its statements and actions will have a uniting significance only if they have a clearly Christian, that is also Christ-centered, implication.

Only Christ-centeredness will be able to avoid the one-sidedness, the ambiguity, and the straight hypocrisy which unfortunately characterize "consensus statements" in the political world. Without Christ-centeredness, political involvement is *divisive* because the world outside of Christ is hopelessly and basically divided. Modern democracies sometimes find ways of dealing with this divisiveness through "separation of powers" and other "checks and balances." But *our* unity, as well as the ontological unity of Christ itself, is in *Christ*, not in political "balance." The real tragedy of divided Christendom is that it does not yet agree on what "unity in Christ" means.


*Conclusion*


"Confessing Christ Today" will be a major theme of the ecumenical dialogue at the Fourth Assembly of the World Council. The mere adoption of such a theme represents a response to the widespread criticism that the ecumenical movement has departed from its original Christian concerns. It represents a remarkable opportunity for an articulate Orthodox witness. How often in the past years have we Orthodox theologians felt quite helpless in expressing our true beliefs and our true feelings, not only because we were unprepared and unaware of Western theological developments, but also because the *framework* of the debate made the Orthodox witness extremely difficult! Now the situation is changing. We are being asked to express what we mean by "confessing Christ." We are expected to express our views clearly, without surrendering to foreign problematics, speaking in a way which can be understood. The temptation of speaking in generalities, repeating well-known formulae, is always strong among us. It gives us a sense of security, but it also keeps us out of the dialogue. We should not be afraid this time to say clearly what we feel. The dialogue is placed on a ground which has always been ours. Our Western brethren expect a challenge from us.

This challenge, I believe, could be expressed in concise and even *critical* statements, which, however, imply a deeply positive content (like St. Cyril's *Anathematisms* against Nestorius). These should include: (1) A clear confession of the divinity of Christ and of the reality of the Incarnation as an event transcending and overcoming the "fallen" historical process, which therefore loses its power to determine Christian ethics. Christians are *free* from the events and ideologies of the world. They can recognize their practical legitimacy, but they are *never bound by them.* (2) An affirmation that man is a theocentric being, called to "deification," and that "secularistic" anthropologies are not only incomplete but plainly wrong. (3) The conclusion (which, of course, has always been made by the Orthodox) that Christian unity can only be found in a joint acceptance of the fullness of the divine gift of God to man, not in minimalistic and reductionistic schemes that accept divisiveness and call it "pluralism."

In my opinion, such an Orthodox contribution to the ecumenical discussion may contribute to salvaging it at a time when so many people, both inside the Orthodox Church and outside of it, have lost confidence in ecumenism.

# 8

# The Unity of the Church and the Unity of Mankind*

The "main theme" of this article is an outcome of developments which took place in the ecumenical movement at large, in the World Council in particular, and, more specifically, in Faith and Order during the past decade.

The definition of the "unity we seek" as a "churchly" unity, the ecclesiology of the New Delhi "unity statement," the trinitarian "basis" adopted in New Delhi for World Council membership, were greeted by some as great victories of the "catholic" tradition in the ecumenical movement. They undoubtedly contributed to greater involvement of Orthodox churches in WCC work, since they gave them the impression, or perhaps the naive illusion, of a return to the "sources" of biblical and patristic Christianity.

Others felt, however, that the adoption of formal theological statements, or the description of unity in biblical or theological terms unrelated to the present historical moment, were nothing more than a futile academic exercise leading the ecumenical movement to a tragic impasse. Their feeling was strengthened when the Fourth Faith and Order Conference in Montreal (1963) failed in an attempt to define the

*Paper delivered on August 3, 1971, at the session of the Commission on Faith and Order, World Council of Churches, meeting in Louvain, Belgium, as an introduction to the main theme of the session. At the time the author was chairman of the Commission. Published originally in *St. Vladimir's Theological Quarterly* vol. 15:4 (1971), pp. 163-77.

ecclesiological nature of the World Council of Churches, proving implicitly that biblical and traditional definitions of church unity were still inapplicable to Christians in their present state of division and that the World Council, when it comes to precise statements and definitions, is still very much bound by the Toronto statement of 1948. No understanding of unity can presently be assumed by all, and if some formulae can be widely accepted, one can be sure that they are understood differently among the WCC constituency. It is this impasse which leads many away from Faith and Order altogether. Faith and Order, whose work was largely responsible for producing the above descriptive formulae, has a reputation as a highly segregated club of hair-splitting professors detached from the real needs of man.

Thus, already in Montreal, a clear shift of emphasis began to take place, a shift which has been described as a move "from God to man," or from "theology" to "anthropology." The intention of this shift was not, expressedly, to modify the basic goal of ecumenism, but to discover the meaning of "churchly" unity in the light of God's plan for all of creation and for man as such. No Christian theology can deny the legitimacy of this new approach if it is based upon a valid methodology in studying the *humanum*. For indeed the Christ-event took place in order to save *man* in the fullness of his developing and creating potentialities, and not simply in order to create an institution following a proper "faith and order." It is certainly not the Orthodox who can object to this anthropological approach to problems of unity. Didn't they inherit from the Greek Fathers a doctrine of the "image of God" in man, an image which no sin is able to erase totally? Didn't St. Maximus the Confessor teach that creation is a dynamic and "energized" being, which Christ assumed in its fullness so that it may again *act* in accordance with its proper design, restoring the entire cosmos in a united harmony? The Christian Gospel is about the fate of all creation and of the whole of mankind, not just about Christians and their institutions.

What "man," what anthropology, was taken as the basis

for the shift we have just mentioned? A simple answer to this question is probably impossible, but one cannot deny that the so-called "secular" categories were decisive in shaping much of recent ecumenical thinking—categories which are, or are presented to be, *common* to both the Christian and the "secular" man. Herein lies precisely the problem which we face. Which anthropology do we choose as criterion in our shifted Faith-and-Order thinking? Is it the "secular" one which "assumes" according to the much misquoted phrase of Bonhoeffer that "there is no God" or is it the anthropology called "theological" by Karl Rahner, which defines man not only as a psychologically "religious" being, but also as a phenomenon impossible to explain without referring to God?

Since the present article does not pretend to be a balanced "presidential" statement or study document, I will allow myself at this initial point to rely mainly on personal judgement. First of all, it seems to me that so far the results of the "shift" to anthropology have not yet contributed much to the ecumenical movement and the cause of Christian unity. They have created a conservative backlash among churchmen without, however, convincing many people in the secular world that the ecumenical movement really has much to contribute to solving "secular" problems. In the Orthodox world they have strengthened the position of those who believe that the Orthodox should withdraw from the ecumenical movement altogether. For them membership in the WCC becomes synonymous with national and international politicking, which may help some Orthodox ecclesiastical institutions in their struggle for survival by providing them with an international forum, but which has nothing to do with the quest of *ecclesial* unity as the Orthodox understand it. Sectarian fringes, both in Protestantism and in Orthodoxy, receive a great boost from this situation.

This judgement, of course, refers to the public image of the World Council as a whole more than to that of Faith and Order. But what place does Faith and Order occupy in the overall image of the Council? Even if one forgets about the recent (and fortunately discarded) possibility that it be dissolved in the broader framework of a new divisional struc-

ture, and even is one acknowledges the constructive theological work which has never stopped being produced in Faith
and Order, it remains obvious that what Faith and Order
represents has largely been overshadowed by noisy talk about
various social causes, most of them justified and valuable
but still peripheral to the main issue of the Christian faith,
the ultimate and eternal destiny of man.

I do not think that anyone will doubt that the various
forms of social utopianism which have monopolized the
enthusiasm of the young and of the not-so-young in recent
years have lost their impetus. Not that the fundamental as-
piration for justice, brotherhood, and peace has disappeared,
but the greater and deeper dimensions of the quest for justice and peace have been much more widely recognized, especially by the young. This recognition leads everywhere to a
new sense of religious experience, to the realization that
man's happiness can be found not only in an equal distribution of material goods, and not even necessarily in social and
political equality and dignity, but must also be attained in
mystical religious experience, often expressed through mu-
sic, through visual arts, through poetry, and through other
forms of *aesthetic* contact with reality. These things form an
*escape* from the monotonous and inhuman determinism of
economics and all other "systems" which pretend to regulate
human life.

In one of his most brilliant short essays, Nicholas
Berdyaev defines every capitulation before this determinism
as "spiritual *bourgeois.*" Whether a capitalist or a socialist,
the spiritual *bourgeois* is unable to say, with Ecclesiastes, "I
have seen everything that is done under the sun; and behold,
all is vanity and a striving after wind" (Eccl. 1:14).
Berdyaev concludes, "The *bourgeois* spirit wins every time
when, among Christians, the City of the earth is mistaken for
the City of heaven, and when Christians stop feeling as pil-
grims in this world."[1]

I am afraid that if Berdyaev had lived until 1968, he
would have found the Uppsala Assembly very *bourgeois* in-

[1] *O Dukhovnoi Burzhuaznosti,* in *Put',* No. 1, Paris (March-April 1926),
p. 13.

deed. However, I have not referred to him to condemn the new emphasis on man in the ecumenical movement as a whole, and in Faith and Order in particular. The fact that we are called to deal with an "anthropocentric" theme in Faith and Order, gives us a new opportunity to salvage the ecumenical movement in a period of acute crisis. It is certainly not by simply returning to a study of ecclesiastical formulae and institutions in themselves, of their historic authenticity and possible adaptability through compromise, that Faith and Order will fulfill its mission fully, but by showing that what is at stake is *man himself*, his life and salvation. The task we have before us today is to answer two questions as spelled out by Leslie Newbigin: "What is the form of church order which will effectively offer to all the *human beings* in this place the invitation of Jesus Christ to be reconciled to God through Him?" and, "What is the form of church order which will effectively offer to *mankind as a whole* this same invitation?"[2]

These questions are indeed Faith-and-Order questions, because the "invitation" comes not from man, not from "history," not from "secular society," but *from Christ*. To restate this is Faith and Order's duty in the WCC. The questions also call us to agree on the meaning of such terms as "human being," "mankind," and "church." To understand what "man" and "mankind" mean we must indeed be attentive (critically, of course) to what the secular world has to say. To agree on the meaning of "church" is admittedly quite difficult, but our ecumenical commitment requires that we continue to listen to each other, and also to our respective pasts, with continuous and brotherly attention.

To initiate discussion, I will limit myself to a few observations on the "unity of the Church," "the unity of mankind," and on "eschatology" in the anthropological context of our main theme.

---

[2]"Which Way for 'Faith and Order'?" in *What Unity Implies* (World Council of Churches, Studies 7, Geneva, 1969), p. 118.

## I. *Man and the Unity of the Church*

The innumerable ecumenical documents on "unity" produced since the beginning of the ecumenical movement have
rarely paid attention to the fact that the recognized polarity
between various ecclesiologies implies differences in the understanding of man's nature. Meanwhile, an understanding
of who man is is essential in order to answer the first of
Newbigin's questions on the relationship of church order to
concrete *human beings*. Let us take, for example, the perennial debate on unity as a *given* reality, as opposed to the
unity which is yet to be realized among divided Christians.

It is well known that in Eastern patristic thought man
is conceived not as an autonomous being, but as being fully
himself only when he is in communion with God. His *nature*
is determined by his being an image of God. Interestingly
enough, there was never a debate in the East concerning the
Pauline use of *pneuma* and its application to both the human
"spirit" and the divine "Spirit," coming from God. This
usage, which embarrasses so many modern theologians because it goes against their presuppositions on "nature" and
"grace" as distinct realities, was not a problem at all for
Irenaeus, who simply affirms that man is by nature made up
of "Spirit, soul, and body," meaning by that that a *divine*
presence is indeed what makes man truly himself (*Adversus
haereses* V, 6, 1). Whether later theologians adopted a more
Neoplatonic language to define the same reality (Gregory
of Nyssa, for example, spoke of the "divine spark" in man),
or whether they started to distinguish between the human
*pneuma* and the Holy Spirit in order to maintain the original
"parenthood" between God and man, they developed the
theology of the *imago Dei* as living communion and always
took for granted that man's *nature* and *ultimate destiny* is
life "in God," or deification (*theosis*).

Needless to say, this understanding of man also implies
that God is "participable," that by creating man He has established between Himself and creation a living and personal link to which He Himself is personally committed, that
it is always possible by looking at man as His image to see

God Himself, that *through* man God is always somehow visible. The image, of course, has been distorted through a mysterious tragedy which happened in creation and which is described through the story of Genesis 3, but it has also been restored through the death and resurrection of Jesus. In Christ the fullness of divinity abides "bodily" and can be seen, accepted, and participated in again. Therefore, it is also in Jesus that one discovers what man authentically is, for Jesus is fully God and fully man, and the one is ("hypostatically") inherent in the other.

In the light of his anthropology, what is the *koinonia* and the "unity" of the Church? Obviously and primarily a unity of man *with God*, and only secondarily a unity of men with each other.

If man is a "theocentric" being, any unity outside the "Center" will be defective and perhaps demonic. "A human being," writes Karl Rahner, "is a reality absolutely open upwards; a reality which reaches its highest (though indeed 'unexacted') perfection, the realization of the highest possibility of man's being, when in it the Logos himself becomes existent in the world."[3] The true *koinonia* occurs when such an "opening" is really possible. In an essay on ecclesiology published posthumously, Vladimir Lossky also insists on this same anthropological dimension. No Christian ecclesiology, he maintains, is possible on the basis of a secularized anthropology, which necessarily reduces the Church to the level of a human organization.[4]

Understood in this sense, *koinonia* is also necessarily a *personal* event. To quote Lossky, "Christ becomes the sole image appropriate to the common nature of humanity. But the Holy Spirit grants to each person, created in the image of God, the possibility of fulfilling the likeness in the common nature. The one lends His hypostasis to (human)

[3]"Current Problems in Christology," *Theological Investigations*, I (Baltimore, 1965), p. 183.

[4]"Catholic Consciousness. The Anthropological Implications of the Dogma of the Church," *St. Vladimir's Theological Quarterly* vol. 14 (1970), pp. 188-189.

nature, the other gives His divinity to the persons."[5] The *koinonia*, as communion of "persons" with God and with each other, implies a theology of the Spirit which concerns the nature of the Christian faith itself.

Pentecost saw the birth of the Church, the *koinonia*, which will gradually acquire structures and will presuppose continuity and authority. It was also an outpouring of spiritual gifts *liberating* man from servitude, giving him personal freedom and personal experience of God. The *koinonia* must uphold this polarity of the faith as continuity and as personal experience. The Spirit authenticates the ministries which are in charge of continuity and authority; but the same Spirit also maintains prophetic functions and reveals the whole truth to each member able to "receive" it. Thus the life of the *koinonia* cannot be reduced either to the "institution" or the "event," either to authority or freedom. It is a "new" community created by the Spirit in Christ, where true freedom is recovered in the spiritual *koinonia* of the Body of Christ.

The conception of the *koinonia*, based upon a "theocentric" anthropology has certain implications.

[a] Communion with God cannot, as such, be "divided." It can only be incomplete and deficient on the personal human level because of man's lack of receptivity to the divine gift. The existence of the *koinonia* in history is the effect of God's action in Christ. It is an openness of God, responsive to the openness of man. A very great Byzantine mystic of the eleventh century, St. Symeon the New Theologian, wrote that those who deny this fullness of revelation close heaven which Christ opened for us and block the way which He Himself has traced out for our return."[6] The Orthodox continue to react violently today when they are told that the Church (i.e. for them the *koinonia* with God) is "divided," i.e. does not exist in its fullness and accessibility anymore.

[b] The fullness of *koinonia* exists only in Christ and is

[5]*The Mystical Theology of the Eastern Church* (London: James Clarke and Co., 1957), pp. 167-168.

[6]Basil Krivocheine, ed., *Syméon le Nouveau Théologien, Catéchèse* I. Collection "Sources chrétiennes," 96, Introduction (Paris, 1964), pp. 39-40.

*given* in the Eucharist. Its "acceptance" by man, until the *eschaton*, is proportionate to his free "openness" to the gift and is therefore always limited. No individual member of the Church can take his membership in the *koinonia* for granted. Actually he is constantly in and out, either excluded through his sins, or reintegrated through repentance. But the ministries, the structures—the entire "Church order"— are a given reality, inasmuch as they are functional to the Eucharist. The *charismata* required by the Eucharist cannot as such be limited. However, as soon as "order" becomes an end in itself, it blasphemously creates a new obstacle to the *koinonia*. Such a blasphemy can be institutionalized, permanently or only temporarily, whenever the structures (episcopate, primacies, etc.) are used for any other purpose than that which is theirs, i.e. to administer, to secure, and to promote the *koinonia* of man with God and in God with his fellow man. Some of us will see such a misuse of the church "structures" whenever they are conceived as vicarious powers, exercised individually *over* the eucharistic *koinonia*. All of us, I hope, will condemn the divisive use of "structures" in the defense of nationalistic, political, racial, or economic interests. And all of us have sins on our conscience in this respect. No one, I think (and certainly not the Orthodox!), could affirm that his belonging to the *Una Sancta* is based upon the actual performance of the ecclesial "structures" of the Church to which he belongs.

Obviously, the eucharistic understanding of *koinonia* will imply that it is the local sacramental community which is its full realization. Union with God in Christ does not require the geographic universality of the *koinonia*. Theocentric anthropology and union *in Christ* make the traditional term of "catholicity," with all its implications and dimensions, more able than others to express the "wholeness" and the cosmic dimensions of salvation in Christ. Indeed, each local community must be the *catholic church*, i.e. understand not only its own internal unity, but also its unity and solidarity with the work of Christ in all ages and in all places. If our anthropology is really "theocentric," if our understanding of *koinonia* is truly eucharistic, the local community is indeed the place where the initial and fundamental Christian experience takes place. However, the *catholicity* of that experience makes it the foundation and the beginning of a responsible, and truly universal mission, which in turn requires proper organization and proper structures.

This theology of unity, based on a particular understanding of man and on a definite meaning of the Eucharist, presupposes that the local community, as it empirically exists, provides the proper experience of that which it is supposed to be. In this respect, the situation is indeed tragic, for different reasons in different places. Among some of us the eucharistic worship is often reduced to frozen ceremonial. Among others the sweeping reforms of the past years have been based either on no theology at all, or else on a theology of the "secular" which practically excludes the *paschal*, liberating character of the Eucharist, i.e. the idea that the *koinonia* which it creates leads us *out of* the world in order that we may return into it as "new creation." It is indeed the duty of Faith and Order to continue the worship study begun at Uppsala. For if the Eucharist is a sacrament of unity, one should unavoidably ask the question: unity in what? The answer can only be: unity in faith and in hope, i.e. as fellow-citizens, by anticipation, of the coming Kingdom of God, for only as such can we overcome division and conflict, which are the inevitable conditions of life "in this world."

## II. *Man and the Unity of Mankind*

The second of Leslie Newbigin's questions was: "What is the form of church order which will effectively offer to *mankind as a whole* the invitation of Jesus Christ to be reconciled to God through Him?" On the other hand, the Uppsala Assembly stated that "the Church is bold in speaking of itself as the sign of the coming unity of mankind."[7] Obviously, the answer to the question, and the meaning of the

[7]*The Uppsala Report*, Report of Section 5 (Geneva: WCC, 1968), p. 17.

statement, again depend upon how we understand "man," and what we mean by "unity."

If we accept as normative the *theocentric* anthropology of Irenaeus and Rahner, and understand church unity as basically a eucharistic and therefore eschatological reality, our attitude will be different from that which considers the Church as immanent in the world, so that its destiny is determined by the secular goals of mankind.

In past years, great emphasis was placed on an understanding of christology and of salvation in universal and cosmic terms. Christ and the Spirit were understood as acting in the whole world, in history, in social change, in revolutionary movements, in world religions, so that it is by "listening to the world" that man can hear God's voice. In opposition to the traditional pietistic and emotional meaning of "renewal," Uppsala discovered "new creation" in the "new things" happening in the world.

Naturally, no Christian theologian has ever denied that the Christ-event has a universal and cosmic significance. Least of all will an Orthodox theologian object to universalist christology. For his own tradition, with Maximus the Confessor, has taught him that man is a microcosm and that Christ, the New Adam, has manifested a new and authentic humanity in which the divisions and contradictions of the fallen world are transfigured and overcome.[8] The Orthodox eucharistic liturgy clearly expresses the same universalism. It is, each time, offered "on behalf of all and for all"—κατὰ πάντα καὶ διὰ πάντα—an expression to be understood in line with the Pauline concept of τὰ πάντα, the whole of creation, as it is dependent upon God, the *pantokrator*. The Eucharist is certainly not offered for Christians alone (although it is indeed *presented by* the committed members of the Church: "*We offer* unto Thee Thine own of Thine own"—Τὰ σὰ ἐκ τῶν σῶν σοὶ προσφέρομεν).

However, modern universalist christologies, as well as the understanding of the Church which is based on them,

---

[8]See the recent book on Maximus by Lars Thunberg, *Microcosm and Mediator. The Theological Anthropology of Maximus the Confessor* (Lund, 1965).

overlook two crucial aspects which are just as fundamental as universalism: the reality of freedom and the reality of evil.

(1) Dependence upon the "elements of this world" is the fate of man unless he *chooses* to recover the dignity God wants him to possess. This is indeed the message of Paul in Galatians: "Formerly, when you did not know God, you were in bondage to beings that by nature are no gods; but now that you have come to know God, or rather to be known by God, how can you turn back again to the weak and beggarly elemental spirits, whose slaves you want to be once more? You observe days, and months, and seasons, and years! I am afraid I have labored over you in vain" (4:8-11). I do not think that anyone can doubt that the concept of the "world," and therefore for us the concept of "secular mankind," is associated in the New Testament with slavery and dependence. Therefore, if the Church must "serve" the world and "unite" mankind—and it certainly exists for that purpose—it can do so only if it is *free from them*, i.e. if it is fully independent from its categories and laws, whatever partial and temporary value they may have. The command to "withdraw from the world," as it is expressed in the New Testament, is primarily a withdrawal from "lust," from dependence upon creaturely beings. It is not a condemnation of the world as evil or an escape from reality. However, no action *upon* the world and in the world is possible without first, a *liberation*.

Christian freedom is not merely a "freedom from" the world; it is also a positive experience and a positive dignity. It is not only a power to choose, but also the very likeness of God in man, unattainable except by communion with God. Once this communion is given, the world cannot take it back. In this sense Christian freedom is the joy and the dignity of the slaves, of the persecuted, of the deprived, and of the humiliated, in other words of all those who are the victims of this world, of its power, and of the determinism from which Christ freed man when He died on the Cross, and its meaning is best understood by those who are themselves suffering from the powerful.

Finally, Christians must recognize the freedom of the "secular" man. For even if "secular" man is, according to Galatians, still enslaved to the powers of the world, he certainly continues to possess the freedom to reject Christ and to refuse His Gospel. The cosmic christologies and secular ecclesiologies of our time all risk annoying the secular man with their *de facto* triumphalism, a triumphalism which assumes a Christian content in the words and actions of those who do not want anything to do with Christianity. It is out of respect for the secular man that a Christian should not impose upon him his own understanding of human destiny.

(2) The reality of evil is another aspect of the situation which is being overlooked. Not that the evil *phenomena* of human life are not recognized, whether they be war, racism, social injustice, or totalitarian oppression; but a *theology of evil* is tragically lacking. I submit that it is impossible to understand the meaning of the Christian faith about man and the world, that it is impossible to be faithful to the significance of the Cross of Jesus, without admitting that Evil has a personalized existence, and therefore a strategy, a sense of reacting and plotting against God's work. Divisiveness and simulation are its major tools. This personalized evil should not be avoided as a problem when one is concerned with the unity of mankind. For, indeed, it possesses the devious talent of entering through the back door precisely when one thinks one has taken a major step towards unity.

Personally, I think that the rationalistic disbelief in Satan is one of the saddest and most unnecessary results of the modern demythologizing of the New Testament narratives, and also one of the most *bourgeois* products of our modern secularized mode of thinking, inherited from nineteenth-century positivism. Writers and artists, especially since Dostoyevsky, have had a much better grasp than theologians of the tragic, cosmic struggle in which man is engaged. What this struggle means practically for us is that unity, in order to be true and authentic, must be *exorcised*; and that exorcism is the preliminary condition, as in traditional rites of baptism to authentic life in Christ. Until the *parousia*, history is a battlefield on which Good and Evil meet. Their

respective forces are confused and the external results of the
battle are always uncertain. In this context it is extremely
important to recognize that on the secular level (and we are
always part of the secular order except in the Eucharist)
our practical choices are not between absolute Good and
absolute Evil. We always have to choose a "better" solution
or even the "lesser evil." The ethical absolute is impossible
on the secular level, and those who are seeking it are in fact
seeking the Kingdom of God. They are, indeed, blessed;
but it is our duty to warn them against utopianism and to
help them discover the Kingdom where it really is.

Absolute achievements, absolute victories, as well as absolute defeats, happen only on the spiritual level; and neither
these victories nor these defeats are necessarily recognized
in the "world." The Gospel is indeed not a success story,
and Christ does not promise success to His disciples. His
own achievement consisted of "disarming the principalities
and powers" (Gal. 2:15), not in revolutionizing the world
and making it sensibly better than it was before. It is certainly our duty to be fully involved in the world and with
the world in seeking both the "better" solutions and the
"lesser evils," but in doing so it is also our duty to be inspired not only by well-known biblical texts which speak of
the universality of salvation, but also by the wise Ecclesiastes:
"What does man gain by all the toil at which he toils under
the sun?" (Eccl. 1:3). By adding some detachment and
some humor to our deadly serious ecumenical documents, we
will make them, in any case, more palatable to the average
reader and certainly more balanced theologically and less
triumphalistic. Political ideologists and doctrinaries may certainly be disappointed by this approach; but we can safely
say, after listening to the millions of young people around
us, that the time for dogmatic political ideologies is *passé*
for most of them. What they are seeking is not one more
radical ideology, but a Truth which is *human*. And what is
more human than the Gospel of Jesus Christ?

As Christians, we are not the first ones to think of the
"unity of mankind" in its relation to the "unity of the
Church." Starting with Constantine and continuing through-

out the Middle Ages the Christian Church, both in the East and in the West, abandoned the eschatology of the early period and considered that the Kingdom of God was not only to be "expected," but also to be *built*. There was no possible division between the "secular" and the "sacred." Redemption was indeed brought to the *whole* of mankind, and consequently, mankind was to be united not only in a sacramental communion, but also as a single society where the whole of life was to be guided by the Gospel. These discoveries of medieval Christianity were correct in their own way and some are still valid today. But now that the Constantinian period is over we generally recognize where it was *theologically wrong:* i.e. (1) in thinking that the authority of Christ could be identified with the political *power* of the state, and (2) in considering that the *universality* of the Gospel is definable in political terms. Today, we are ready to celebrate the burial of Christian empires and states, but have we really abandoned the mistaken aspects of their theology? To ask this question is to imply that the theology of many of our "secularists" is actually the theology of Constantine, Justinian, and Hildebrand, although the means at their disposal are different and, consequently, the methods they propose to use are different as well. But the *main* concern is the same. They want to define Christianity in such a way as to solve the problems of this world, to be "relevant" in terms understandable to "secular man," and practically, to use secular means to attain a goal which has been set by others. But then what about Jesus' answer to Pilate: "My kingdom is not of this world; if my kingdom were of this world, my servants would fight" (John 18:36) ? What about the demonic which constantly tempts us (whether we are rich or poor, oppressors or oppressed) with power, with bread, and with easy, "miraculous," i.e. utopian, solutions?

Christianity has suffered enough because it identified itself with power, with the state, with money, with the establishment. Many of us rightly want to disengage it from these embarrassing allies. In order to win its true freedom *the Church must become itself again, and not simply change camps.*

To help our churches in this task is the *raison d'être* of
Faith and Order. Without fear of dialectical conflict among
us, or between us, or between us and others, honestly dis-
agreeing if necessary, let us be bold enough to speak our own
mind. We are indeed at a historical moment when Faith and
Order is asked not simply to give its expertise on refined
theological issues, but to say its word on the concern of all.
This word should give a true Christian meaning to our necessary and actually unavoidable involvement in promoting
and helping this world, this society, this humanity, to become
more just and more human. Where else can this meaning
be found except in the light of a sound eschatology?

### III. Eschatology

The unity of the Church and the unity of mankind will
ultimately and fully coincide only in the fulfillment of the
Kingdom of God, *and not before.* Only in this perspective
can one legitimately say that the unity of the Church is an
anticipation of the unity of mankind. In the Eucharist, however, it is possible to taste the very reality of future unity,
which is not simply a human reconciliation and fellowship,
but a unity in God, in the fullness of truth, in the joy of the
Kingdom. As such, the Eucharist, as well as the entire liturgical worship which constitutes its framework, can legitimately be considered as an *escape* from the determinism of
the world, from our animal existence which ends in death,
from the limitations and the frustrations which we meet
as Christians in the world. Liturgical worship is indeed the
leisure, the "going home" of Christians inasmuch as they are
through their baptism the citizens of the Kingdom of God,
not of the world. The anticipated eschatology of the
Eucharist is a relief, the very experience of a victory already
won, which gives credit to Christ's words: "In the world you
have tribulation; but be of good cheer, I have overcome the
world" (John 16:33). This saying is actually being tested
when Christians are making their "trip" to the Kingdom of
God. We believe that this happens not only emotionally and

subjectively, but quite really, however "hard" this "saying" may appear in the eyes of the world (cf. John 6:30-32).

The Eucharist is not an escape from reality, but from slavery, from the so-called "necessities" of the world, from the "determinism" of rationality. Therefore it is a victory over the "powers and principalities." No wonder that the meaning of worship as *liberation* is best understood by those Christians who are openly rejected by the world, persecuted, oppressed, or segregated—in communist Russia or in the black ghettos of America. I also think that it is *this* kind of worship which will eventually be understood by all who today are in the midst of an authentic quest for the "disestablishment" of Christianity.

The Eucharist, therefore, as an eschatological event is the "place" of unity. However, Christ is not only the *Omega*, the goal of history, but He is also the *Alpha*. The beginning and the end are both in Him. This implies that for Christians the "last things" will not be as entirely "new" as they will be for the world. The Judge of the "last day" is already our recognized Master. Thus the Church holds to the "apostolic" faith both because it is through the apostles that she knows about the acts performed by Jesus and because the apostles will sit on twelve thrones judging the twelve tribes of Israel. The maintenance of an "apostolic" structure of the Church is not only a conservative reaction (however legitimate conservatism may be), but also an eschatological necessity. Only those "structures" of the Church are truly necessary which have an eschatological dimension. Those of us who, for example, insist on the necessity of an "apostolic" episcopate must also show the episcopate to have an eschatological significance. It is not simply a practical requirement in reference to the "world." The *Alpha* and the *Omega* are one; and it is to this oneness, to this unity, that Christ promised indestructability from the gates of Hell.

Now if the Eucharist is the eschatological event *par excellence*, it is for and through the Eucharist that one discovers what in church structure is truly eschatological and therefore necessary for the Church to be the Church. It is on this point that the perennial debate between East and

West has taken place. Is a *universal structure* of the Church really necessary, although it is obviously not determined directly by the Eucharist (as is the structure of the local church with a bishop at its head)? Is there an eschatological necessity for the universal Church to be structured around a universal "vicar of Christ"? Is the "successor of Peter" only in *one* particular church, or is there one in every local community which is through the Eucharist the *catholic* Church, i.e. the fullness of the Church in that place?

Obviously the debate on this point is theologically the same as the one on the history of the Church and the unity of *mankind*. The Eucharist can only be celebrated locally, but it is celebrated for the whole world. And also, having made their trip to the Kingdom of God, Christians are indeed being sent into the world in order to prepare it to become the Kingdom of God. For that purpose they must act together, use the means which the world offers, be understood by the secular man, and, on a deeper ontological level, *assume* the world as God's creation. We know also that this assumption includes even "the sins of the world" for the sake of the world's redemption.

The medieval Western Church thought that the proper way of realizing these goals, including that of uniting mankind, was to assume state powers over the world. It also presumed that Christ Himself had provided the universal Church with a structure adapted to the needs of the secular world. The East, meanwhile, was largely relying on the (supposedly) Christian state to take care of the secular tasks, limiting its ecclesiology to the eschatological eucharistic dimensions. Modern "secularists" rejecting the idea that the Church has a God-given structure, think that it must learn from the world how to make that world better.

The theological and practical mistakes of these three attitudes are rather clear. But to find alternatives in this rapidly changing world of ours is harder than to criticize the mistakes of others.

Our difficulties lie in the polarization and chaos which have characterized the theological developments in the Western world during the past decade. There are certainly hopes but still no clear evidence that these iconoclastic years will have cleared the way for a renewal of Christian experience and real witness. Our difficulties lie also in the fact that, called to speak of the "unity of mankind," we are ourselves not at all free from the forces which actively divide it, and therefore cannot pass a clear judgement upon these forces. Some of us are able to judge the fault of other societies, but the conditions in which we live would not allow us to direct the same judgement closer to home. Others, on the contrary, are fascinated by the problems which assail the social groups to which they belong, so that they are unable to see these problems in the wider perspective of a world society. The result of these limitations is that our statements often lack the ultimate Christian integrity which would impart lasting significance and deserve respect.

These are the reasons why my goal in these preliminary remarks has been to discuss the basic theological presuppositions which would allow us to move into the concrete issues which face us. Do we believe that the eschatological Kingdom is anticipated in a unique and fundamental way through the Eucharist in the local community, and that a Eucharist-centered Church is our primary responsibility as a starting point of an active involvement in the service of the world (which is certainly desirable, but not always possible, and, at times, ineffective and even harmful)? If our answer is positive, we will basically agree with Jacques Ellul when he castigates the illusion "that justice can be attained by a political organization of any kind"[9] and believes "that it is only through complete refusal to compromise with the forms and forces of our society that we can find the right orientation and recover the hope of human freedom."[10]

If we disagree with the letter of Ellul's judgement, and know through our own experiences in our own local situations that active work for reconciliation, unity, and justice is actually possible *through involvement*, are we ready to admit that the results achievable through such an involvement will

[9]*The Political Illusion* (New York: Knopf, 1967), p. 191.
[10]*Ibid.*, p. 203.

possibly be a "lesser evil" only, and, as such, of no great eschatological significance?

If we disagree totally with a Eucharist-centered eschatology, what safeguards do we offer against utopianism? Do we mean that the better world which the young people of all continents seek will come about through any of the world religions other than Christianity, or through a combination of several of them, or through any of the ideologies which presently compete for men's souls?

A clear answer to these questions, or at least to some of them, would be a useful signpost for a truly meaningful debate on the issues facing us in the ecumenical movement.

# 9

# The Orthodox Church
# and Mission:
# Past and Present Perspectives*

The purpose of this paper was to introduce a discussion between Orthodox and Episcopalians, rather than to cover all the problems connected with mission. I will limit myself to three points:

(1) An Orthodox reaction to recent development in the theology of mission.

(2) The theological and practical issues involved in the Orthodox Church's mission in the West, and particularly in America.

(3) The present perspectives of the Orthodox-Anglican dialogue in the light of the points made in (1) and (2), and as a continuation of recent theological exchanges.

In (1) and (2) I will attempt some Orthodox "soul-searching." Point 3 will contain a practical proposal.

## I. Development in the theology of mission

Until recently Christian mission was generally understood in a fairly simple way. It consisted of an organized and in-stitutionalized effort to expand the membership of the various Christian churches and denominations among those who did

*Paper delivered at a session of the Anglican-Orthodox Consultation, held at St. Vladimir's Seminary, on April 21, 1972, and published originally in *St. Vladimir's Theological Quarterly* vol. 16:2 (1972), pp. 59-71.

not belong to them. Throughout the nineteenth century most Protestants—not to speak of the Roman Catholics and the Orthodox—took for granted that the denomination to which they belonged was indeed the "true Church," and that it was fully legitimate to proselytize everywhere, among non-Christians as well as among members of other Christian groups.

Such a simple and straightforward concept of the Christian mission led on the practical level to two consequences of major importance:

(1)  Direct competition existed between Christian missionaries in the so-called "mission lands," i.e. primarily the countries of Africa and Asia where Western European countries extended their colonial empires and where missions thus became possible. This competition constituted a serious handicap to the progress of Christianity. The "younger churches," being nothing but branches of European church organizations, became bound by post-Reformation theological and institutional categories, and were obliged to import the white man's factionalism, adding it to their own racial and tribal divisions.

(2)  Protestant and Roman Catholic proselytism extended to the Christian East, especially the Middle East and India. Totally unsuccessful among Moslems, Western missionaries justified their assignments to Middle Eastern countries by turning towards the economically and intellectually "underdeveloped" masses of Eastern Christians, Orthodox or Monophysite. As a defensive reaction against this proselytism—which actually started in the seventeenth and eighteenth centuries with the active support of Western diplomats and money—Ecumenical Patriarch Cyril V issued his well-known synodal decision in 1755, declaring the invalidity of all sacraments performed by Western Christians and, therefore, requiring the reception of converts through baptism.[1] This decision superseded the earlier practice of accepting the Western converts through chrismation. It was

---

[1] The texts relative to that decision can be found in J. D. Mansi, *Sacrorum Conciliorum Nova et Amplissima Collectio*, ed. L. Petit, vol. 38, cols. 576-640.

accepted in the standard Greek canonical collection known as
*Pedalion*, or *Rudder*, and is considered as binding even today
by some Orthodox conservative circles, especially in Greece.
One should also note that active proselytism among Orthodox was also widely practised by Western churches on the
American continent. It remains active even today on the part
of conservative-fundamentalist groups (for example among
the Alaska natives).

At the time of the big missionary expansion of the Western European churches in the nineteenth century the Church
of Russia was the only one in the Orthodox world able to
engage in a similar undertaking. It did so on the territory of
the Russian European and Asian Empire, but also beyond it.
The mission to Japan was most successful, under the leadership of the recently canonized St. Nicholas Kasatkin (†1913);
and missionary activity was not interrupted in Alaska after
its sale to the United States in 1867, or in other parts of the
American continent. This Russian missionary activity was
not restricted to non-Christians, but also welcomed Roman
Catholics and Protestants. These Russian missions followed
the principles accepted in Byzantine times, i.e. they were based
on a liturgy translated into the various vernacular languages.
Thus, the Orthodox liturgy was celebrated in dozens of
Asian dialects; Scripture was also translated[2]

It is among the Protestant missionaries that the idea of an
"ecumenical movement," which would stop missionary competition and make possible a unified Christian witness to the
world, took its initial shape. It was based upon the realization by the theologians that unity and mission are inseparable
in the New Testament's understanding of the Church. Being
practical men, those responsible for the various missionary
boards and organizations also understood what could be
gained by cooperation and sharing of resources.

[2]It is useless to refer here to the very extensive literature available in
Russian on the Orthodox missions; easily accessible general surveys are
available in E. Smirnoff, *Russian Orthodox Missions* (London, 1903), S.
Bolshakoff, *The Foreign Missions of the Russian Orthodox Church* (London,
1943), and also in J. Glazik, *Die russisch-orthodoxe Heidenmission seit
Peter dem Grossen* (Münster-Westf., 1954) and *Die Islammission der rus-
sisch-orthodoxen Kirche* (Münster-Westf.: 1959).

This missionary impulse was a constant element in the
ecumenical thinking of the first half of this century. It cul-
minated in the merger of the World Council of Churches
and the International Missionary Council at the Assembly
in New Delhi (1961).

Since that time the "turbulent 'sixties" brought a radical
change in prevailing ideas about mission, and therefore of
the ecumenical movement itself as well. The idea that there
was a "Christian world" sending missionaries to evangelize
the "pagans" was discarded totally and replaced with a new
global theology of mission which properly assumed that the
Church's mission could not be restricted to some geographical
areas or mission lands at a time when the entire world had
become "secular." Less properly it also proclaimed a "secular
understanding of Christianity." Christian mission was now
identified with involvement in those historical processes which
were presumed to be "progressive," i.e. promoting a better
human life. Christians were called to abandon their traditional concentration on Scripture and worship and to "listen
to the world." "The Secular" was defined as a source of
continuous revelation, and the mission of the Church was
to consist in helping those causes and ideologies which were
struggling for "peace" and "justice." The major problem in
the newly prevailing understanding of mission was that it
practically excluded any concept of "peace" and "justice"
except the "secular" ones, that it followed the fads and
utopias of current sociological trends, and that it betrayed
the *basic content* of the Christian Gospel, which is about
eternal life, resurrection, and the Kingdom of God, i.e. realities impossible to define in sociological, "secular," or political terms.[3] The culminating point for the progress of these
ideas on mission was the Conference on Church and Society
(Geneva, 1966) and the Fourth Assembly of the WCC
(Uppsala, 1968). Since Uppsala, militant secularism seems
to be subsiding, with the "secular world" itself (whatever
that term means) apparently more receptive to irrational
pentecostalism and emotional religious revivalism than to the
dry utopias of political activists.

[3]See above, Chapter 8.

Through its involvement with the various ecumenical agencies, the Orthodox Church was in constant touch with these developments in the Christian idea of mission. One should honestly recognize that so far it has had a rather negligible influence upon the outcome of the various debates on mission. Perhaps history will show, however, that the serene immutability of Orthodox worship, the sort of passive immunity which has been shown so far by the mass of the Orthodox people (the contradictory attitudes of a few "professional ecumenists" notwithstanding) to theological fads and slogans, will prove to have been ultimately an effective witness—something deeper and greater than conservatism for conservatism's sake. It is clear that the Orthodox understanding of the Christian Gospel and of the Church is very difficult to reconcile with either the pre-New Delhi or post-New Delhi prevailing concepts of mission.

The Orthodox would, of course, readily agree that (1) mission belongs to the very nature of the Church, which is called "apostolic" both because it carries on the apostolic faith and because it is being sent into the world as the apostles were to witness to Christ's resurrection; (2) mission cannot be reduced only to preaching the Gospel; it implies service, i.e. witness through deeds as well as words.

These two points imply that a Church which ceases to be missionary, which limits itself to an introverted self-sustaining existence, or, even worse, places ethnic, racial, political, social, or geographic limitations upon the message of Christ, ceases to be authentically "the Church of Christ." Also, since Christ was "anointed to preach the good news to the poor" and "sent to proclaim release to the captives" and "to set at liberty those who are oppressed" (Luke 4:18), it is clear that His Church must do the same.

However, the Orthodox cannot but disagree with the ecclesiological presuppositions which would be behind the integration of mission into the structure of ecumenical organizations, such as the World Council of Churches, because these are associations of *divided* Christians. The Orthodox hold the Orthodox Church to be the one undivided (i.e. theologically and biblically *indivisible*) Church, and consider any association of divided "churches" as nothing but an *ad hoc* attempt to work for the unity of Christians, or as a means of cooperation in fields where cooperation is possible, including some forms of proclamation of the Christian Gospel to the world. However, *mission*, in its ultimate theological meaning, is an expression of the *Church itself*. It cannot grow out of a divided Christendom, but only from the One Church; and it leads to conversion to this One Church.

The Orthodox obviously will also disagree with the "secularist" interpretation of mission. The goal of mission is an acceptance of the Gospel which *liberates* from the determinism of secular categories, i.e. "the world." A Johannine text has always served as the basis of the "missionary" dimension in ecumenism "that they way all be one; even as thou, Father, art in me, and I in thee, that they also be in us, so that the world may believe that thou hast sent me" (John 17:21). This speaks of a *divine* unity which is also to become the unity of men, and which is something which the world "cannot give." This is precisely the reason why true unity of Christians is realized not in common action, not even in common witness to those outside, but in the *closed* sacramental mystery of the *Eucharist*. It is only because the Eucharist is an eschatological event, an anticipated advent of the Kingdom to come and a fullness of divine presence, that it is also unifying. This is also why any form of "intercommunion"—i.e. eucharistic communion between Christians who are divided in faith and in ultimate ecclesial commitment—necessarily *reduces* the Eucharist to a form of human fellowship, distinct from the union in the Kingdom of God which is the Eucharist's ultimate meaning.

I personally believe that there is general agreement among the Orthodox on the positions described above. However, for a variety of non-theological reasons, the Orthodox have failed to act with sufficient consistency and logic. For example, they accepted the integration of the World Council of Churches and the International Missionary Council in New Delhi (1961), even if several of them voted against it at the Assembly. The reason for such an accommodating spirit was that since the Russian Revolution the Orthodox Church has had very little possibility to engage in an organized missionary effort, so the hierarchies of the various Orthodox churches did not feel any practical threat on this point from the proposed integration. On the other hand, many Middle Eastern prelates were happy with the idea of having Protestant missionaries somehow controlled through an organization of which the Orthodox themselves were members.

Similarly, one can certainly say that the Orthodox reaction against the "secularized" concept of mission would have been stronger if the tragic situation of the Moscow Patriarchate did not compel it to participate in the various "progressive" organizations of the Western world, which are considered as useful by the Soviet Government provided they are silent about the defects of Soviet society and vocal only in criticizing the West.

These and other practical considerations are hardly conducive to a consistent Orthodox witness. I believe, however, that it is our particular responsibility as Orthodox Christians of the West to make a truly positive and useful contribution to the current theological debate in world Christendom about the nature of mission.

## II. Orthodox mission: East and West

Until the beginning of this century, the Orthodox Church was closely associated with the national tradition of those East European countries which were part of what historians recently labeled the "Byzantine Commonwealth":[4] Greece, Bulgaria, Serbia, Romania, and Russia. From Byzantium they all inherited a social system which implied the alliance between Church and State. On the other hand, the traditional Byzantine missionary approach, immortalized by Sts. Cyril and Methodius in the ninth century, consisted of translating both Scripture and liturgy into the vernacular. This led to the creation of Christian nations which integrated Christianity deep into their ethnic and cultural experience. New Ortho-

---

[4]Dimitri Obolensky, *The Byzantine Commonwealth: Eastern Europe 500-1453* (New York: Praeger, 1971).

dox ethnic-religious groups continued to appear until our own times: in Poland, in Czechoslovakia, in Albania, as well as in Asia, where Russian missions were in progress.

Since nineteenth-century nationalism was a fundamentally *secular* phenomenon, the Orthodox world, in adopting it, passed through its own peculiar experience of "secularism." The Church often became directly involved in causes which a particular ethnic group considered as "holy," even at the expense of the national interest of others. Examples of ecclesiastical nationalism are numerous and shameful.

In spite of it all, however, the *framework* of national life was still largely determined by Orthodox Church Tradition. The mission of the Church was understood clearly as a preservation and expansion of that Tradition, along with the national and social life of the various so-called "Orthodox nations." The mission of the Church, as part of a "Christian civilization," developed a social and personal ethos which had itself been shaped by Orthodox Christianity.

This situation was not without ambiguity because it frequently led to confusion between Church and civilization, religion and nation. It was radically changed, however, by the Russian Revolution and the establishment of Communist states in countries of Eastern Europe. Driven into a ghetto, administratively persecuted, prevented by law from exercising any influence on society, the Church struggles for survival as a closed worshipping community. The historical future of the Orthodox Church, as a world communion, depends upon the result of that struggle.

But the Russian Revolution also resulted in a dispersion of Orthodox Christians throughout the world, and this dispersion gave a totally new dimension to Orthodox mission. In this new "diaspora" were many theologians and intellectuals who, especially in Western Europe, contributed much to the Orthodox witness in the ecumenical movement.

In terms of numbers, however, it is in America that the Orthodox presence is most sizable. Most Orthodox communities here were founded not by political anti-communist émigrés, but by immigrants from Central and Eastern Europe, as well as from Greece and the Middle East. They came here

in the nineteenth century by their own free will and in order
to build a new permanent life for themselves and their children. Thus, for the first time since the Great Schism and the
Reformation, Orthodox Christians were permanently sharing
a country, a language, a culture with their Roman Catholic,
Anglican, and Protestant brethren.

The role of the "churches" in shaping American society
is, of course, well known. Denominations coincided with
the ethnic and economic *strata* to which the various groups
belonged.[5] On the other hand—and this is especially true of
the Orthodox—church-belonging signified token-faithfulness
to the old country and served as a tool of ethnic identification
and fellowship. As distinct from classical European confes-
sionalism, the "denominationalism" of America was not
doctrine-oriented. It never excluded forms of "non-denom-
inational" religious experience: revivalistic, pentecostal, pantheistic, deistic, or national. But the American religious scene
was also rich in "sectarian" phenomena, reacting against broad
denominationalism through exclusiveness, fanaticism, and big-
otry. The Orthodox Church could accept neither the "denominational" nor the "sectarian" patterns of American religion
for itself. It claimed to be the true "Catholic" Church, excluding ecclesiological relativism, but also assuming the responsibility and the mission of "catholicity." This sense of
responsibility and mission, which clearly distinguishes "the
Church" from a "sect," implies openness to everything true
and good anywhere. Thus, by establishing itself permanently
in America, the Orthodox Church was confronted with the
difficult challenge of remaining true to its catholic self-
understanding in a pluralistic society, without becoming either
a denomination or a sect.

The original diocese established on the American continent in Alaska in 1840 was canonically dependant upon the
Russian Holy Synod in St. Petersburg. It remained ecclesiastically under Russia after the sale of Alaska to the United
States in 1867, when it extended its jurisdiction and activities
to the entire continent, its center being transferred first to San

---

[5]It is sufficient to refer here to R. H. Niebuhr's classic, *The Social Sources
of Denominationalism* (New York: Meridian Books, 1957).

Francisco (1872), then to New York (1903). A major par-
ticularity of that diocese was that it was always multi-ethnic
and multi-lingual. Immigrants from the Russian Empire
proper constituted a very small minority in its midst. It always
called itself a "mission," i.e. a mission first to the natives of
Alaska, who had their native clergy and worshipped in their
own tongues, and second to the Slavic "Uniate" immigrants
from Austria-Hungary, who returned to Orthodoxy in hun-
dreds of thousands once they were established in America.
The diocese also welcomed into its midst Orthodox immigrants
from all countries. An Arab, Raphael Hawaweeny, was consecrated auxiliary bishop in New York. In 1905, Archbishop
Tikhon presented to the Holy Synod of St. Petersburg a report containing a proposal for an independent American
Church, which would, however, recognize the identity of the
various ethnic groups.[6]

Without idealizing the picture (for indeed, there were
inconsistencies and shortcomings) one can say that the policies
of that original Orthodox diocese of America were at that time
faithful, at least in intention, to the truly catholic aspect of
the Church's mission. It was only after the Russian Revolution
that the Orthodox mission in America disintegrated. New
waves of immigrants organized themselves ecclesiastically on
a purely ethnic basis, in spite of a few prophetic voices, like
that of Ecumenical Patriarch Meletios Metaxakis, who spoke
of the establishment of an "American Orthodox Church" in
his enthronement address in 1921.[7]

Indeed, overcoming ethnic divisions and acting truly as
one Church is the precondition for a meaningful Orthodox
witness in the West, especially in America. But the ultimate
problem lies on an even deeper level. Is Orthodoxy intrinsically the "Eastern" form of Christianity? Or, conversely, is
Christianity fundamentally and culturally inseparable from
the East? An affirmative answer to the latter question would
imply that to be a Western Christian or a Western Orthodox
is, to say the least, a great handicap in one's spiritual progress,

[6]English text of the main passage of the report in *St. Vladimir's Theological
Quarterly* vol. 5:1/2 (1961), pp. 114-115.

[7]An extract of the address in English, *ibid.*, p. 114.

for true Christianity and "the West" are actually incompatible. Those among the Orthodox who adopt that position and rationalize it in terms of practical behavior, reduce Orthodoxy to the sectarian pattern of American religion. One simply *cannot* be both Orthodox and American, but one has to become—at least culturally and spiritually—a Greek or a Russian. However, quite often this identification of Orthodoxy with Eastern cultural or ethnic patterns also leads to a practical "denominationalism." Some people believe that since one cannot reasonably expect to have Western Christians transformed into Greeks or Russians, one should try to coexist with them peacefully, sharing the common interdenominational deism of American religion. This corresponds to the so-called "unity without union" pattern in ecumenism. Thus, paradoxically, ethnicity naturally allies itself either with "sectarianism" or with "denominationalism," because it constitutes, first of all, a negation of the catholicity of the Church.

Thus, a definition of the Orthodox mission in the West today requires, first of all, a clear understanding of what catholicity means, what is implied by a truly *catholic church life*—which is more than a conceptual definition of the third "attribute" of the Church.

It should be understood, first of all, that catholicity does not imply bland cosmopolitanism—a renunciation of the cultural diversities, identities, and peculiar "talents" of nations, civilizations, or ethnic groups. The Cyrillo-Methodian pattern of creating national churches without imposing upon them external linguistic conformity was a direct application in the field of mission of the miracle of Pentecost, and therefore the best possible witness to catholicity.

Yet once Christianized, nations, languages, and cultures accept the common criterion of catholicity and cease to be mutually exclusive. The Byzantine Orthodox hymnography for the day of Pentecost is entirely built on the biblical theme of the opposition between the story of the tower of Babel ("the tongues divide men from each other") and the miracle of the tongues in the upper room ("the *same* Spirit" speaks in the languages of all nations). Catholicity therefore implies comprehensiveness: not indifference and individualism, but a comprehensiveness built upon the universality of redemption. The Orthodox claim of being the "Catholic" Church involves the Church's mission to the world, a world which has been redeemed by Christ in its wholeness. The Church, therefore, cannot be "Eastern" or "Western" in its very nature if it is to remain the Church of Christ.

There is a fundamental sense, however, in which the New Testament revelation implies history and geography. The Incarnation took place in history, and the establishment of the Church involved concrete people—Jews and Greeks—who belonged to the civilization of their own time. They were not twentieth-century Americans. The historical uniqueness of the Christ-event presupposes that no other moment of history but the time of Jesus of Nazareth was "the fullness of time" described and explained in the writings of the New Testament. It also presupposes that the Incarnate Son of God was the Jewish Messiah, and that the universality of life and salvation was to be revealed nowhere else but in Jerusalem. Also, if one holds a belief in Tradition, one accepts that the Church, as the new temple and the vehicle of the Spirit, has taken the right options and given the right definitions of doctrine throughout its history. These definitions are also historically and geographically qualified. Our task today is then to remain *consistent* to these options and definitions of the past, even when we are called to develop them, or to take totally new options relevant for the issues of our own time.

There is an important sense, therefore, in which our mission today as Orthodox Christians cannot be uprooted from the tradition of Eastern Christianity, where the fullness of the Christian Tradition has been carried through centuries of history, the Tradition of the Greek Fathers in particular. A true sense of our mission must also recognize that catholic Tradition has had in the past expressions other than the Greek or the Russian, and that any reduction of Christian truth to a particular historic form presupposes a reduction of catholicity itself. The Greek Fathers expressed Holy Tradition not because they were Greek, but because they lived the Church's catholicity, which was also lived by others and should be relived anew by us in the twentieth century.

It is not my purpose in this paper to attempt a definition of the "Christian West" from the point of view of Orthodox ecclesiology; and this does not seem to be the main point when one is concerned with Christian mission in a country like America, which can hardly be considered a Christian country anymore. America challenges the Orthodox Church with problems which it never had to face before, and this challenge is, frequently, a challenge to the Christian faith itself. I believe that Orthodox Tradition is particularly explicit on some fundamentals which our society could discover to be directly relevant, such as a Trinitarian view of God, a "theocentric" understanding of man, and an ecclesiology based on communion, rather than on authority.[8] If only Orthodox mission and witness could be more consistent in practice than they are with these fundamentals of the Orthodox faith! Orthodoxy could assume a crucial responsibility in reshaping Western Christianity at a moment when the secular activism of the 'sixties is subsiding and when people are more ready than before to understand the language of prayer, of contemplation, of experience, and may thus become concerned again with the truth for its own sake. On the other hand, one can say that an American Orthodox Church, invested with freedom and dynamism learned in the West, can have a "mission" to the mother churches of the Orthodox East, where freedom does not exist and dynamism is impaired by law or custom.

### III. Orthodox and Anglicans

Relations between Anglicans and Orthodox have a long history, which involves not only theology, but also British, Ottoman, Russian, Greek, and other politics. To a degree this is still the case today in some of the aspects of the "dialogue" on the world scale. By contrast here in the West, and particularly in America, we have the opportunity and the responsibility to envisage our relations within the framework of a society which is common to us, and of concrete problems which our churches face.

[8]See below, Chapter 10.

A generation ago an opinion widespread among Episcopalians and shared by some Orthodox was that the inevitable
Americanization of East European immigrants would cause
them to be gradually absorbed into the Episcopal Church.
Although some examples of such absorption exist, the pattern has clearly failed to materialize. On the contrary, there
exists on the part of the Orthodox a defensive reflex against
ecumenical mergers, which generally becomes even more pro-
nounced with the progress of Americanization.

Perhaps the theological and ecumenical developments of
the last decade have created a new and more fruitful stimulus
for an Orthodox-Anglican rapprochement. With the spectacular changes which have occurred in Roman Catholicism
on the one hand, and the widespread so-called "secularization" of theology, many values which the Anglican tradition
stood for, even when it was reluctant to formulate them with
theological precision, are being questioned in an unprecedented way. What is at stake is not so much this or that
minute issue of "church order," but the very nature of the
Christian faith and of the Church's mission.

Much too frequently Anglican-Orthodox dialogues, always very "ecclesiastically" oriented, have dealt with issues
like apostolic succession, the number of sacraments, church
authority, etc., without much reference to the existential requirements of Christian life and mission. Perhaps uninten-
tionally, the participants on both sides often gave the impression that it was possible to settle issues of ecclesiology or
sacramental theology, without sharing a common experience
of the nature of Christianity and its mission.

Whatever one thinks of the theological and ecclesiastical
developments of the last decade, one must recognize that the
current debate is about the *nature of Christianity*, and not
only about its institutional or sacramental expressions. Now
if Orthodox and Anglicans, or at least some of them, could
try to reach a meaningful agreement on what the Christian
Gospel really means, they might subsequently be able to move
forward towards an evaluation of the real state of our inter-
church relations as well.

Personally, I consider the debate on the pages of our

*Quarterly*, which involved John Rossner, Bishop Maguire, and Georges Barrois,[9] as a quite significant beginning, precisely because it transcended the usual ecclesiological entanglements of the Anglican-Orthodox dialogues. Let us talk—at least for a while—about the Trinity, Jesus Christ, and the nature of man, not simply repeating the formulations of the past, but testing each other's concrete preaching and teaching on these basic truths of Christianity. In order to be successful, such a conversation must involve those who are really involved and responsible for the life of our congregations, not only professional ecumenists.

The conversation can follow the model set by the "Fellowship of St. Alban and St. Sergius," still the most lasting and the most influential forum of the Anglican-Orthodox rapprochment, and can be organized quite unofficially without either the direct involvement, or the exclusion of ecclesiastical leadership. Whether one should follow Bishop Maguire's suggestion of composing together a "twentieth-century statement of common faith and practice"[10] is a matter of debate. Bishop Maguire is careful enough to specify that his plan is not to prepare "the sufficient doctrinal basis for a merger," but rather a "guiding-device in our own further on-going conversations." However, Professor Barrois is rightfully afraid of formal "Confessions." The Orthodox seventeenth-century experimentation with writing "Confessions" in response to Protestant requests was ultimately helpful to no one.[11] It seems to me that what really is important is the methodology to be followed. The question is whether it is possible to provide today's Christians with a rallying

[9]John Rossner, "Orthodoxy and the Future of Western Christianity," *St. Vladimir's Theological Quarterly* vol. 14:3 (1970), pp. 115-135; Kenneth Maguire, "Comments on Anglican-Orthodox Relations," 15:4 (1971), pp. 178-190; Georges Barrois, "Anglican-Orthodox Relations: Reflexions of an Orthodox on some Anglican Comments," *ibid.*, pp. 191-211.

[10]*Op. cit.*, p. 189.

[11]For a good contemporary evaluation of the role of the seventeenth-century Orthodox "Confessions," see S. Harakas, "Creed and Confession in the Orthodox Church," *Journal of Ecumenical Studies* vol. 7:4 (1970), pp. 721-743; an even more critical evaluation is Basil Krivocheine's article, "Is a New Orthodox Confession of Faith Necessary?" *St. Vladimir's Seminary Quarterly* vol. 11:2 (1967), pp. 69-72.

point around the Gospel of the resurrection of Christ, and its
implications:

— the divinity and the humanity of the One Christ,
  i.e. the doctrine which affirms that the ultimate
  destiny of man is in God, and also that God can
  manifest Himself in man and through man;

— the experience, in Christ, of the Father and the
  Spirit, i.e. of a God whom we experientially discover as Trinity;

— the *paschal* understanding of the life of the Church,
  whose saving mission in the world consists in *freeing*
  man from the world's determinism and in restoring
  his *communion* with God.

The question whether an agreement on such points as
these will contribute or not to further inter-ecclesiastical relations can be left to divine Providence to decide. Actually,
I believe that theological work of this kind will be useful
only if it does not fall into the usual trap of institutionalized
ecumenism: the drafting of ambiguous documents serving to
prepare, promote, or anticipate institutional mergers without achieving a real meeting of minds. Instead of composing documents aimed at satisfying professional ecumenists,
let us test our ability to say something together to the un-
believer, or even to the rank and file church member. If we
were able to discover, at some point, that we actually preach
the *same Gospel*, it would be easier for us to handle the out-
standing ecclesiological issues as well.

I know that some of my skeptical Orthodox brethren will
say that it is always easy to find an agreement with a select
group of Anglicans and thus have the illusion of Anglican-
Orthodox understanding, while in reality the Anglican communion will remain based on an all-inclusive comprehensiveness, and other Anglicans will, simultaneously, be agreeing
with Methodists and Presbyterians. It seems to me, however,
that the overall theological situation is changing in this re-

spect too. The Anglican communion is approaching a moment of truth. To it falls the option of a merger with the main-stream of liberal Protestantism, and it has sometimes the feeling that Rome does not need it anymore as a "bridge" to Protestantism—so many Roman Catholics have crossed the river on their own!

But the moment of truth is coming for Orthodoxy also. The ethnico-political structures which provided it with a sense of continuity are crumbling rapidly. Only its truth and catholicity can preserve its credibility to the young men and women of today.

It is not the time, then, for both Anglicans and Orthodox to make an attempt to meet each other in the truth of the Gospel?

# 10

# Orthodox Theology Today*

One of the major developments in the history of Christendom is the breaking down in the present century of linguistic, cultural, and geographical boundaries between Christians of the East and West. Only fifty years ago contacts between them were possible only in the form of polemical confrontations in areas where Orthodox and Roman Catholics had so identified their ecclesiastical with their national allegiances that meaningful theological dialogue was made impossible. The picture is radically changed today in two major ways.

(1) Both Eastern and Western Christianities are now present almost everywhere in the world. More particularly, the intellectual witness of the Russian diaspora in the period between the two world wars, and the gradual maturing of an American Orthodoxy after the Second World War, have greatly contributed to bringing the Orthodox Church into the mainstream of ecumenical events.

(2) The challenge of one single and radically secularized world confronts all Christians. This challenge has to be faced as a problem needing a theological and spiritual answer. For the younger generations everywhere, it is immaterial upon *which* spiritual genealogy this answer depends, Eastern or Western, Byzantine or Latin, provided it appeals to them as Truth and Life. Orthodox theology, therefore, will be either truly "catholic," i.e. relevant for everyone, or

*Originally published in *St. Vladimir's Theological Quarterly* vol. 13:1/2 (1969), pp. 77-92.

it will be no theology at all. It must define itself as "Orthodox theology," not as "Eastern" theology, and it can do so
without renouncing its "Eastern" historical roots.

These obvious facts of our contemporary situation do not
imply at all that we need what is commonly called "new
theology," which breaks with Tradition and continuity; but
unquestionably the Church needs theology to solve *today's*
problems, not to repeat ancient solutions to ancient problems. The Cappadocian Fathers are great theologians because they succeed in preserving the content of the Christian Gospel when it was faced with the challenge of the
Hellenic philosophical world view. Without their partial
acceptance and partial rejection of this world view, but first
of all without their *understanding* of it, their theology would
be meaningless.

Our task today is not only to remain faithful to their
thought, but also to imitate them in their openness to the
problems of their age. History itself has driven us away
from cultural limitations, provincialism, and ghetto mentality.


# I

What is the theological world in which we live and with
which we are called into "dialogue?"

"*Against* Pascal I say: The God of Abraham, Isaac, and
Jacob and the God of the philosophers is the same God."
This central affirmation by Paul Tillich, reflecting his concern for bridging the gap between biblical religion and
philosophy, is followed by a recognition of the limits of man's
power of knowing God. Tillich also writes: "[God] is a
person and the negation of Himself as a person." Faith,
which for him is undistinguishable from philosophical knowledge, "comprises both itself and the doubt of itself. The
Christ is Jesus and the negation of Jesus. Biblical religion
is the negation and the affirmation of ontology. To live
serenely and courageously in these tensions and to discover
finally their ultimate unity in the depths of our own souls

and in the depth of divine life is the task and the dignity of human thought."[1]

Even if contemporary radical theologians often criticize Tillich for what was, according to them, his exaggerated concern for biblical religion, he expresses the basic humanistic trend to which they also belong: the ultimate religious truth is "in the depth of one's soul."

What we see in contemporary Western Christian thought is a reaction against the old Augustinian dichotomy of "nature" and "grace," which determined the entire history of Western Christianity in the Middle Ages and since. Even if St. Augustine himself was able to fill the ontological gap between God and man by having recourse to a Platonic anthropology, attributing to the *sensus mentis* a particular ability to know God, the dichotomy to whose creation he contributed so much dominated both Scholasticism and the Reformation. Conceived as an autonomous being, fallen man has been seen as unable not only to save himself, but also to produce or to create anything positive without the help of grace. He needed the help of grace which would create in him a "state," or *habitus*, and only then his acts would acquire "meritorious" character. Relations between God and man were thus conceived as extrinsic to both. Grace could be bestowed on the basis of the "merits" of Christ, who by his redemptive grace had given satisfaction to the divine justice which had previously condemned man.

While rejecting the notions of "merit" and "good works," the Reformers remained faithful to the original dichotomy between God and man. They even emphasized it more strongly in their understanding of the Gospel as a free gift of God opposed to the absolute powerlessness of fallen man. The cheap "means of grace" distributed by the medieval Church are thus replaced by a proclamation of mercy by an all-powerful transcendent God.

Protestant Barthian neo-orthodoxy gave a new impetus to this fundamentally Augustinian intuition of the Reformers. But today's Protestant theology is in sharp reaction against

[1]Paul Tillich, *Biblical Religion and the Search for Ultimate Reality* (Chicago: The University of Chicago Press, 1955), p. 85.

Augustinism. Karl Barth himself, in the last volumes of his *Kirchliche Dogmatik*, drastically changes his original position, best expressed in his *Römerbrief*. He reaffirms the presence of God in creation, independent of the Incarnation. He thus himself reflects the new mood in theology, that which we find in people as different as Paul Tillich and Teilhard de Chardin, and out of which springs the more radical and less serious American "new theology" of Hamilton, Van Buren or Altizer.

We will return below to the ontology of creation, presupposed by Barth and by Tillich. Let us note here in passing its obvious parallelism with both the essential preoccupations and the conclusions of the Russian "sophiological" school. If, as it has been noted, several later parts of Barth's *Dogmatics* could have been written by Father Sergius Bulgakov,[2] the same can be said, for example, of Tillich's christology, which, like Bulgakov's, defines Jesus as an expression of eternal "God-manhood."[3] The parallelism with Russian sophiology and the common background of the two schools of thought in German idealism are obvious. If Florensky and Bulgakov had been one generation younger, or if their works had been better known, they would certainly have shared Tillich's and Teilhard's influence and success.

"Sophiology" offers today hardly any appeal to younger Orthodox theologians, who prefer to overcome the nature-grace dichotomy along christocentric, biblical, and patristic lines. But in Protestantism the philosophical approach to Christian revelation dominates the scene. It comes to the fore simultaneously with another revolution which happened in an area necessarily quite crucial for Protestants: biblical hermeneutics.

The Bultmannian and post-Bultmannian insistence on the distinction between Christian *kerygma* and historical facts is

[2]See for example *Church Dogmatics*, IV, part three, first half, translated by G. W. Bromiley (Edinburgh: T. and T. Clark, 1961), pp. 461-478 (on eschatology and "apocatastasis"), and S. Bulgakov, *Nevesta Agntsa* (Paris, 1945), pp. 581-586 (in Russian).

[3]Paul Tillich, *Systematic Theology* (Chicago: The University of Chicago Press, 1957), II, p. 148.

another way of subjectivizing the Gospel. For Bultmann the Christian faith, instead of being provoked, as the traditional view would hold it, by the witnesses who saw *the risen Lord* with their own eyes, is, on the contrary, the true *origin* of the "myth" of the Resurrection. Thus one has to interpret it as only a natural subjective function of man, a *gnosis* without objective criteria. If one accepts that any fact scientifically uncontrollable—such as the Resurrection—is *ipso facto* an unhistorical myth and that the created order is therefore unchangeable even by God, one in fact postulates a deification of the created order, a determinism obligatory to God Himself and therefore willed by Him. Revelation can therefore occur only through this same created order. God can only follow the laws and the principles He Himself has established, and knowledge of revelation is not qualitatively different from any other form of human knowledge. The Christian faith, to use Tillich's expression, is then only a "concern for the Unconditional," or for the "depth" of created Being.

For Tillich, of course, as well as for Bultmann, the historical Jesus and his teaching remain at the center of the Christian faith. "The material norm of systematic theology today," Tillich writes in *Systematic Theology*, "is the *New Being* in Jesus as the Christ as our ultimate concern."[4] The problem is, however, that against the general framework of their thought Jesus can be chosen as "ultimate concern" only arbitrarily, for there are no objective and compelling reasons for us to select him for that position. If Christianity is defined only in terms of a response to natural and eternal longings of man for the Ultimate, there is nothing which can prevent this response from leading elsewhere than toward the historical Christ.

Such a substitution is obviously occurring, for example, in William Hamilton. "The theologian," he writes, "is sometimes inclined to suspect that Jesus Christ is best understood as neither the object nor the ground of faith, neither as person, event, or community, but simply as a place to be, a standpoint. That place is, of course, alongside the neighbor,

[4]*Ibid.*, I, p. 50.

being for him."[5] Metamorphosed into a post-Hegelian and post-Marxist "social-mindedness," the Christian love for the neighbor thus provides the Tillichian "ultimate concern" and becomes practically undistinguishable from left-wing humanism.

Extreme radicals of the Altizer-Hamilton-Van Buren type represent only a small minority among contemporary theologians, and a reaction against what they represent is in the making. However, the nature of this reaction is far from being always healthy. It sometimes amounts to a simple recourse to traditional authority: the *magisterium*, in the case of Roman Catholics, and the Bible, understood fundamentalistically, in the case of Protestants. Both require, in fact, a sort of *credo quia absurdum*, a blind faith unrelated to reason, science, or the social realities of our day. Obviously this understanding of authority ceases to be theological and in fact expresses the irrational conservatism which is generally connected with political reaction in America.

Thus, rather paradoxically, both extremes of the theological spectrum agree in somehow identifying the Christian Gospel with the empirical causes of realities—sociological, political, revolutionary—of *this world*. Obviously the old antinomy between "grace" and "nature" is still not resolved; it is rather suppressed either by a simple negation of the "supernatural" or by an identification of God with a heavenly *Deus ex machina* whose main function is to keep doctrines, societies, structures, and authorities as they are. The place of Orthodox theology clearly is in neither of these two camps. Its main function today is perhaps to restate the fundamental biblical theology of the Holy Spirit as the Presence of God among us; as the Presence which does not suppress the empirical world, but saves it; as the one who unites all in the same truth, but distributes a diversity of gifts; as the supreme gift of life, but also the giver, who always remains above all creation; as the sustainer of the Church's Tradition and continuity, but also the one who, by His very presence, makes us truly and ultimately *free* sons of God. As Metro-

[5]William Hamilton, *Radical Theology and the Death of God* (Indianapolis: Bobbs-Merrill Co., 1966), pp. 92-93.

politan Ignatius Hazim said in Uppsala: "Without the Spirit God is far away; Christ belongs to the past, and the Gospel is dead letter, the Church is merely an organization, authority is domination, mission is propaganda, worship is evocation, and Christian action is a slave morality."[6]

## II

The doctrine of the Holy Spirit loses much when it is treated *in abstracto*. This is probably one of the reasons why so little good theological writing is done about the Holy Spirit, and why even the Fathers treat Him almost exclusively either in occasional polemical writings or in writings on spirituality. However, neither patristic christology, nor the ecclesiology of the early centuries, nor the very notion of salvation is understandable without a fundamentally pneumatological context.

I will try to illustrate this point with five examples, which also appear to me as the very issues which make the Orthodox witness relevant to the contemporary theological situation. These five examples are fundamental affirmations of patristic and Orthodox theology.

1. The world is not divine and it needs salvation.
2. Man is a theocentric being.
3. Christian theology is christocentric.
4. True ecclesiology is personalistic.
5. The true conception of God is trinitarian.

### 1. The World is not Divine.

In the New Testament, and not only in the Johannine writings, there is a constant opposition between the "Spirit who proceeds from the Father" (John 15:26), "whom the world cannot receive, because it neither sees Him nor knows Him" (John 14:17), and the "spirits" which must be "tested

[6]Metropolitan Ignatius Hazim, "Behold, I Make All Things New," *St. Vladimir's Theological Quarterly* vol. 12:3/4 (1968), p. 113.

to see whether they are of God" (I John 4:1). In Colossians the entire cosmos is described as controlled by the powers and principalities, "the elemental spirits of the universe" opposed to Christ, although "created through Him and for Him" (Col. 1:16; 2:8). One of the most characteristic novelties of Christianity was what it demystified or, if you wish, secularized the cosmos. The idea that God abides in the elements, in water, in springs, in stars, in the emperor, was totally and from the beginning rejected by the Apostolic Church. At the same time, this same Church condemned every Manicheism, every dualism. The world is not evil in itself; the elements must proclaim the glory of God; water can be sanctified; the cosmos can be controlled; the emperor can become God's servant. All these elements of the world are not goals in themselves, for to consider them as such was precisely what was meant when the ancient pre- Christian world deified them, but they are defined at the very bottom of their existence by their relation to their Creator and also to man, the Creator's image in the world.

This is why all the rites of sanctification, of which the Orthodox Byzantine liturgy (as well as all the other ancient Christian liturgies) are so fond, all include:

[a] elements of exorcism: "Thou didst crush the heads of the serpents which lurked there" (from the Great Blessing of Water on Epiphany day);

[b] an invocation of the Spirit "who proceeds *from the Father*, i.e. not "from the world"; and

[c] the affirmation that in its new sanctified existence matter will be reoriented to God and replaced in its original relation to the Creator, and will now serve *man*, whom God established as master of the universe.

An act of blessing and sanctification of any element of the world thus *liberates* man from dependence on it and puts it at man's service.

Ancient Christianity thus demystified the elements of the physical world. The task of theology today is to demystify "Society," "Sex," "the State," "Revolution," and other modern idols. Our modern prophets of secularization are not all wrong about the secularizing responsibility of Christians—

secularization of the cosmos has been a Christian idea since the beginning—but the problem is that they secularize the Church and replace it with new idolatry, an idolatry of the world whereby man renounces again the freedom which was given to him in the Holy Spirit and submits himself anew to the determinism of history or sociology, of Freudian psychology or utopian progressivism.

## 2. Man is a Theocentric Being.

In order to understand what the "freedom in the Holy Spirit" is, let us first recall a quite paradoxical statement of St. Irenaeus of Lyons: "The perfect man consists in the commingling and the union of the soul receiving the Spirit of the Father, and the mixture of that fleshly nature which also was molded after the image of God" (*Adversus haereses* V, 6, 1). This passage of Irenaeus, as well as its several parallels, is to be evaluated not according to the precisions of post-Nicene theology, for according to that criterion it does present many problems, but in its positive content which will also be expressed, in different terms, by the entire consensus of the patristic tradition. What makes man truly man is the presence of this Spirit of God. Man is not an autonomous and self-sufficient being; his humanity consists firstly in an openness to the Absolute, to immortality, to creativity in the image of the Creator, and secondly in the fact that God met this openness when He created man and that, therefore, communion and participation in divine life and glory is man's *natural* element.

Later patristic tradition has consistently developed Irenaeus' idea (not necessarily his terminology), and this development is especially important in relation to the doctrine of human freedom.

For Gregory of Nyssa, the fall of man consisted precisely in the fact that man fell under the control of cosmic determinism, whereas originally, when he participated in divine life, when he preserved in himself the image and likeness of God, he was *truly free*. Freedom, therefore, is not opposed

to grace and grace, i.e. divine life itself, is neither a way
through which God forces us to obey Him, nor an additional
element superimposed upon human nature to obtain greater
credit for human good works. Grace is the *milieu* in which
man is wholly free. "When a man turns to the Lord the
veil is removed. Now the Lord is the Spirit, and where the
Spirit of the Lord is, there is freedom. And we all, with
unveiled face, beholding the glory of the Lord, are being
changed into His likeness from one degree of glory to another" (II Cor. 3:16-18).

One of the most fundamental presuppositions of this
passage from St. Paul, as well as the anthropologies of St.
Irenaeus and St. Gregory of Nyssa, is that nature and grace,
man and God, the human mind and Holy Spirit, human freedom and divine presence, *do not exclude each other.* On the
contrary, true humanity, in its authentic creativity, in its true
freedom, in its original beauty and harmony, appears exactly
when it participates in God or when, as both St. Paul and
St. Gregory of Nyssa proclaim, it progresses from glory to
glory without ever exhausting either the riches of God or
the potentialities of man.

It is common today to affirm that theology should become anthropology. An Orthodox theologian can, and even
should, accept a dialogue on this basis, provided he adopts
at the very start an *open* view man. The modern dogmas
of secularism, of man's autonomy, of cosmo-centricity, or
sociomagnetism, must first be rejected as dogmas. Many of
these modern dogmas have, as we have already said, very deep
roots in Western Christianity's ancient fear of the idea of
"participation" (which it generally identifies with emotional
mysticism) and in its predisposition to view man as an autonomous being. But these dogmas are fundamentally false.

Even today the prophets of "Godless Christianity" are,
first of all, misinterpreting *man.* Our younger generation is
not "secularistic," it desperately tries to satisfy its natural
thirst for the "Other," for the Transcendent, for the True
One, in such ambiguous escapes as Oriental religions, drugs,
or psychedelic devices. Our age is not only the age of secularism, but also an age of emerging new religions, or sub-

stitutes for religion. This is unavoidable because man is a theocentric being; when he is denied the true God, he creates false ones.

## 3. Christocentric Theology.

If the view of man held by the Fathers is a true one, every Christian theology must necessarily be christocentric. A christocentric theology which is based, as it often has been, upon the idea of extrinsic redemption, of "satisfaction," of the grace of justification being externally added to an otherwise autonomous human existence, is often opposed to pneumatology, for indeed there is no place in it for the action of the Spirit. But if our God-centered anthropology is true, if the presence of the Spirit is what makes man truly man, if human destiny is in restoring *communion* with God, then Jesus, the New Adam, the one man in whom true humanity was manifested because He was born, in history "from the Holy Spirit and the Virgin Mary," is necessarily in the center of theology; and this centrality does not in any way limit the role of the Holy Spirit.

Christocentrism in theology is under heavy attack today on the part of Bultmannian hermeneutics. If every event is a myth unless it follows the laws of empirical science and experience, the "Christ-event" loses its absolute uniqueness, for its uniqueness is, in fact, subjectivized. Nevertheless, christocentrism is still strongly affirmed not only among the remnants of Barthian Neo-Orthodoxy, but also by Tillich. It co-exists in the works of theologians who, like John Macquarrie, attempt to reconcile demythologizing of such events as the Resurrection and the Ascension[7] with a generally classical exposition of theological themes.

However, even in those comparatively traditional or semi-traditional authors one can observe a very explicit taste for Nestorian or adoptionist christology.

Tillich, for example, formally expresses this when he

[7] John Macquarrie, *Principles of Christian Theology* (New York: Charles Scribner's Sons, 1966), pp. 265-267.

writes that without the concept of adoption Christ "would
be deprived of his finite freedom; for a transmuted being
does not have the freedom to be other than divine."[8] What
is evident in this position is the old Western idea that God
and man, grace and freedom, are mutually exclusive. It is
a remnant in Tillich's thought of a "closed" anthropology
which excludes Orthodox christology.

The rehabilitation of Nestorius and his teacher, Theodore
of Mopsuestia, has been undertaken by both historians and
theologians since the last century in the name of the autonomy of man. This rehabilitation has even made some
prominent Orthodox converts, who also show a marked
preference for this "historicity" of the school of Antioch,
postulating that history can be only "human" history. To be
an *historical* being, Jesus must have been not only fully, but
somehow *independently* a man. The central affirmations of
Cyril of Alexandria about the Logos Himself becoming son
of Mary—who is therefore Theotokos—or the theopaschite
formulae officially proclaimed as criteria of Orthodoxy by
the Fifth Council in 553, appear to them as being at best
terminological abuses or "baroque" theology. How can the
Logos, i.e. God Himself, *die* on the cross, according to the
flesh, since God is by definition immortal?

There is no need to enter here into a detailed discussion
of theological concepts related to the doctrine of hypostatic
union. I would like simply to affirm very strongly that the
theopaschite formula of St. Cyril of Alexandria, "the Logos
suffered in the flesh," is one of the greatest existing Christian affirmations of the *authenticity* of humanity. For if the Son
of God Himself, in order to identify Himself with humanity,
in order to become "similar to us in all things, including
death"—human death—died on the cross, He testified in a
manner greater than any human imagination could ever have
conceived that humanity is indeed the most precious, the most
vital, the most imperishable creation of God.

Of course Cyrillian christology presupposes the "open"

[8]Paul Tillich, *Systematic Theology*, II, p. 149. A good critique of Tillich's
position is found in George H. Tavard, *Paul Tillich and the Christian
Message* (London: Burns and Oats, 1962), pp. 129-132.

anthropology of the early and later Fathers; the humanity of Jesus, by being "en-hypostasized" in the Logos, was no less full humanity, because the presence of God does not destroy man. Moreover, one can even say that Jesus was more fully man than any of us. Here again, to quote Karl Rahner (who, among the contemporary Western theologians is on this point the closest to the mainstream of patristic tradition), "Human being is a reality absolutely open upwards; a reality which reaches its highest perfection, the realization of the highest possibility of man's being, when in it the Logos Himself becomes existent in the world."[9] One can also say that a christology which includes theopaschism presupposes *openness* in God's being as well.

It is therefore against the background of *this* christology that one can accept the idea that theology is also necessarily anthropology, and, vice versa that the only true Christian understanding of man—his creation, fall, salvation, and ultimate destiny—is revealed in Jesus Christ, the Logos of God, crucified and risen.

## 4. Personalistic Ecclesiology.

If the presence of the Holy Spirit in man *liberates* him, if grace means emancipation from slavery to the deterministic contingencies of the world, membership in the Body of Christ also means freedom. Finally, freedom means *personal* existence.

Our liturgy teaches us very clearly that membership in the Church is an eminently *personal* responsibility. Catechetical instruction, the pre-baptismal dialogue, the development of the penitential discipline, the evolution of communion practices, all illustrate the *personal* character of the Christian commitment. It is also well known that in the New Testament the term "member" (μέλος), when it designates the Christians as "members of Christ" (I Cor. 6:15) or as "members of each other" (Eph. 4:25), is applied only to in-

[9]Karl Rahner, *Theological Investigations*, I, trans. by C. Ernst (Baltimore: Helicon Press, 1961), p. 183.

dividuals, and never to corporate entities such as local churches. The local church, a eucharistic community, is the *body*, while *membership* in it is an exclusively personal act.

To speak of "personal Christianity" and of "personal" faith is today highly unpopular, largely because religious personalism is immediately associated, in the West, with pietism and emotionalism. Here again we observe the same old incomprehension of the idea of real participation in divine life. When "grace" is either a thing bestowed by the institutional Church or a sort of general gratuitous act bestowed upon all of humanity by God's just and unequivocal omnipotence, the manifestations of personal experience of God become either pietism or emotional mysticism. Meanwhile, there is the tremendous urge of many Christians today to identify their Christian faith with social activism, with group dynamics, with political causes, of which utopian theories of historical development, precisely because they lack that which is the center of the New Testament message, a personal living experience of a personal God. When the latter is being preached by evangelistic revivalists or pentecostals, it indeed often takes the form of emotional superficiliality, but only because it has no basis in either theology or ecclesiology.

It is, therefore, the very particular responsibility of Orthodoxy to realize the tremendous importance of the scriptural and patristic experience of the Church as a body which is both a *sacrament*, i.e. implying an objective presence of God in a hierarchical structure independent of the individual worthiness of the members, and a *community of living free persons* with individual and direct responsibility to God, to the Church, and to each other. Personal experience receives both its reality and its authenticity from the sacrament, but the latter is given to the community in order to make the personal experience possible. The paradox which is implied here is best illustrated by the great St. Symeon the New Theologian, who is perhaps the most "sacramental" of the Byzantine spiritual writers, but who also describes as the greatest heresy ever confessed the opinion held by some of his contemporaries that a personal experience of God is impossible.[10] All saints, both ancient and modern, will confirm that this paradox stands at the very center of Christian existence in the present *aion*.

Obviously, it is through this antinomy between the "sacramental" and the "personal" that one finds the key for the understanding of authority in the Church. Here again, the responsibility of Orthodoxy is almost unique. It becomes increasingly clear today that the problem of authority is not simply a peripheral issue between East and West in the Middle Ages, expressed in the dispute between Constantinople and Rome, but that the tremendous drama of the entire Western Christianity is contained precisely in this issue. An authority, which wrongly considered itself for centuries as alone responsible for truth, has achieved a remarkable success in training the entire Church membership in the virtue of obedience, but meanwhile has liberated it from responsibility. It is being openly challenged today, mostly for the wrong reasons and for wrong causes, while it tries itself to give head-on-battles on untenable positions. In fact, salvation may come not from authority any more, for faith in authority is obviously lacking, but from a theological "restoration." Will Orthodox theology, with its justified claim to have preserved the balance between authority, freedom, and responsibility for truth, have anything to say? If not, the real tragedy will not be in our losing denominational pride, for self-righteousness is always a demonic feeling, but in the consequences which may well result for the Christian faith as such in the world today.

## 5. *The True Conception of God Is Trinitarian.*

A little earlier we mentioned the Cyrillian christological formula—"One of the Holy Trinity suffered in the flesh"— the formula sung at every liturgy as part of the hymn "Only-Begotten Son." We affirmed that it was firstly a recognition of *humanity* as a value sufficiently important

---

[10]*Catéchèse XXIX*, ed. Basile Krivochéine, in the collection "Sources Chrétiennes," 113 (Paris, 1968), pp. 177-179.

for God Himself, important enough to bring Him to the cross;
but this formula also implies a personal or "hypostatic" existence of God.

Objections against this formula are all based upon the
identification of God's existence with his essence. God cannot die, said the Antiochian theologians, because He is immortal and changeless by nature or essence. For them, the concept of "death of God" was such a logical contradiction in terms
that it could not be true, either religiously or philosophically.
At best it was, just as the term *Theotokos* applied to the Virgin
Mary, a pious periphrasis. Meanwhile, in Orthodox theology
the Cyrillian formula has been not only accepted as true, both
religiously and theologically, but made a criterion of Orthodoxy.

God is not bound by the philosophical necessities or attributes which our logics attribute to Him. The patristic notion of ὑπόστασις, which was unknown to Greek philosophy
(it used the word ὑπόστασις in a different sense) and which
is different, in God's being, from His unknown, unknowable, and therefore undefinable essence, implies an openness
on the part of God that makes it possible for a divine person, or hypostasis, to *become* fully man. It meets the
"openness upwards" which is characteristic of man. It makes
possible the fact that God does not stay "up there," or "in
heaven," but that He really comes all the way down to the
human mortal condition, not in order to absorb it or to destroy
it, but in order to save it and to restore its original communion with Himself.

In patristic theology this "condescension" of God occurs
on the level of the personal or hypostatic existence of God.
If it occurred in reference to God's nature or essence—as
some so-called "kenotic" theories have asserted—then the
Logos would, so to say, gradually become less and less God
by approaching death, and cease finally to be God at the
moment of death. The Cyrillian formula implies, on the
contrary, that to the question, "Who died on the Cross?"
there is no other answer than "God," because in Christ there
was no other personal existence than that of the Logos and

that death is necessarily a *personal* act. Only *somebody* can die, not *something*.

"You were in the tomb according to the flesh, in paradise with the thief, on the throne with the Father and the Spirit, O Indescribable One." This is what the Church proclaims in its paschal hymn: a union in one hypostasis of the essential characteristics of both the divine and the human natures, each remaining what it always is.

The human intellect cannot argue against this doctrine by referring to the qualities of divine essence, because this essence is totally unknown and indescribable and because, if we know God directly, it is precisely because the person of the Son assumed *another nature* than the divine, made an *inrush* into created existence and thus spoke with the human mouth of Jesus, died a human death, rose from a human grave, and established an eternal communion with humanity by sending the Holy Spirit. "No one has ever seen God; the only Son, who is in the bosom of the Father, He has made Him known" (John 1:18).

It would obviously be much too easy to establish a parallel between our modern "death of God" theologians and St. Cyril of Alexandria. The context and the purpose of theology there and here are radically different. But it is indeed possible, and for Orthodox theologians quite necessary, to affirm that God is not a philosophical notion, an "essence with characteristics," a concept, but that He is what Jesus Christ is, that knowledge of Him is primarily a personal encounter with the one in whom the Apostles recognized the Incarnate Logos, and also with the "Other One" who was sent afterwards as our advocate in our present expectation of the end, and that in Christ and through the Spirit we are led to the Father Himself.

Orthodox theology does not start with proofs of God's existence, with converting men to philosophical deism. It confronts them with the Gospel of Jesus Christ and expects their free response to this challenge.

It has been often said that the Eastern Fathers, when speaking of God, always start with the three persons, to prove later their "consubstantiality," while the West starts with God as one essence, tries later to suggest also the distinction into three persons. These two tendencies are at the origin of the *filioque* dispute, but they are also of great relevance for the present. God is, in Orthodox theology, the Father, the Son, and the Spirit, as persons. Their common divine essence is totally unknowable and transcendent, and its characteristics themselves are best described in negative terms. But the three act personally; they make their common divine Life (or "energy") participable. Through baptism "in the Name of the Father, of the Son, and of the Holy Spirit" new life and immortality is a living reality and experience, and becomes available to man.

## III.

The Orthodox Church today is being involved through an unavoidable process of history more and more deeply, not only in the so-called "ecumenical dialogue," but also here in the West in the mainstream of social development. This involvement is, unfortunately, not a process that the Orthodox Church is able to control consciously. Let us admit it frankly, the Pan-Orthodox Consultations started *after* all the local churches had already taken decisive steps in favor of participation in ecumenism, and after our churches, our people, our priests, and our laymen were involved in modern social changes. In addition, the entire Orthodox diaspora, and especially the Church in America, which is already an organic part of Western society, find themselves in constant dialogue with other Christians, atheists, and agnostics, whether they want it or not. What we can do now is to reflect on what has already happened. Here only a sound theological revival can avoid a new historical catastrophe for Orthodoxy in our generation. I say "historical catastrophe in our generation" because I believe that the Spirit of Truth cannot permit a catastrophe of the Church as such, although it can obviously tolerate, as it has in the past, catastrophies of individual churches or generations of Christians. Those who want to put theology aside and replace it with sentimental ecumenism,

avoiding the so-called "difficult issues," betray the true spirit
of Orthodoxy. It is indeed theology: biblical, patristic, and
contemporary, that we need. We have to remember that it
was in dialoguing with outsiders—Jews, pagans, heretics—
that the Fathers, the Apostles, and, actually, the Lord Jesus
Himself, developed their theology. Let us imitate them in
this!

At this point I would like to note also that the ecumenical movement itself is going through a period of re-
evaluation which gives, perhaps, to Orthodox theology its
day of opportunity. Whatever happens at the spectacular
meetings between church leaders, however big the noise of
the solemn assemblies, however intelligent the schemes of
ecclesiastical politicians, the average intelligent Christian is
less and less interested in the superficial ecumenism which
they promote. The conservatives shy away from it because
it often implies ambiguity and compromise. The radicals
have no interest because the Church, according to them, has
no real existence as an institution and they formally anticipate
its dissolution. They have no use, therefore, for a universal
ecumenical super-institutionalism and super-bureaucracy.
The future therefore lies in facing together the meaning of
the Christian Gospel in the world. The only sound and meaningful future is with theology, and as I tried to show in my
five examples, the Orthodox witness is often precisely what
people seek, consciously or unconsciously.

It is therefore unavoidable that the Orthodox Church
and its theology define themselves both as Tradition and faithfulness to the past and as response to the present. When it
faces the present, the Church, in my opinion, has two very
concrete dangers to avoid. (1) It must not consider itself a
"denomination," and (2) it must not consider itself a sect.

Both temptations are strong, especially in our own American situation. Those, for example, who identify Orthodoxy
with ethnicity necessarily exclude from church membership,
and even from the range of the Church's interests, anybody
and anything which does not belong to particular ethnic traditions. Now a denomination and a sect have this in common,
that both are exclusive: the first because it is relativistic by

definition, since it considers itself as one of the possible forms of Christianity, and the second because it finds pleasure—a demonic pleasure indeed—in isolation, in separation, in distinctiveness and in feelings of superiority.

We all know that *both* of these attitudes are represented in American Orthodoxy. The function of Orthodox theology is to exclude and to condemn them both. Theology alone, coupled of course with charity, hope, humility, and other necessary components of truly Christian behavior, can help us to discover and to love our Church as the Catholic Church.

The Catholic Church, as we all know, is not only "universal." It is true, not only in the sense that it *has* the truth, but also in that it rejoices when it finds this truth elsewhere. It is for all men, not only for those who happen to be its members today, and it is ready to serve unconditionally every progress everywhere towards the good. It suffers wherever there is error or division, and it never compromises in matters of faith, but it is infinitely compassionate and tolerant of human weakness.

Obviously, such a Church is not a man-made organization. It would simply not exist if we alone were in charge of it. Fortunately, what is demanded from us is only to be true members of the Church's divine head, for as St. Irenaeus has written, "Where the Church is, there is the Spirit of God; and where the Spirit of God is, there is the Church, and every kind of grace; but the Spirit is Truth" (*Adversus haereses* III, 24, 1).

# 11

# The Christian Gospel and Social Responsibility: The Orthodox Tradition in History *

Both theologically and anthropologically, "society" and "culture" are inseparable concepts, and the one-sided approach to human life which reduces all issues to their socio-economic aspects is wrong. It is probably one of the greatest responsibilities of those who accept the Christian Revelation to be able to evaluate and judge history on the basis of a wholesome, or "catholic" view of human life, which includes the demands of the spirit as well as those of the body, inseparably united.

The concept of Tradition needs clarification. It implies a distinction between Tradition, as inner consistency throughout history with the one apostolic faith, and the human "traditions" which reflect the legitimate variety of historical process and at times conflict with the unchanging and unchangeable content of the Gospel. Clearly, Orthodox theology, which emphasizes the importance of Tradition, must always be able to distinguish—especially in the context of the ecumenical dialogue—between Tradition and "traditions." I will try to make this distinction as clear as possible in reference both to ideas and to events of Orthodox Church history.

*Paper delivered at a Lutheran-Reformed-Orthodox Consultation, New York, in Spring, 1975.

The distinction itself, as well as our evaluation of the various human "traditions" as they have existed in history, can be established only on the basis of theological presuppositions derived from the Christian faith. This faith gives meaning to history and provides it with a goal, an *eschaton*. Christian initiatives in the life of society are not blind initiatives; they are based on knowledge of what can ultimately be *expected* as the end of human history and what cannot. Similarly, it is the same *expectation* which provides them with a criterion to judge the initiatives taken by others.

Our discussion of historical developments in the past of Orthodoxy must therefore start with a definition of "eschatological" categories. It is our belief that at least some contrasting developments will become easier to understand if one applies the same eschatological criteria both to the East and to the West.

## I. Three eschatologies

Christianity always rejects the ontological dualism of the Manicheans, and also the idea—common in the Gnosticism of the second century—that visible creation is the work of an inferior Demiurge, distinct from the Transcendent God; instead it affirms the basic goodness of creation, "both visible and invisible." With equal consistency, however, the New Testament maintains an existential dualism between "this world," which is in a state of rebellion against God, and "the world to come," when God will be "all in all." Christians expect "the city to come" and consider themselves as only "sojourners," rather than full-fledged citizens in the present world. However, this New Testament eschatology and its practical implications have been lived and understood differently by Christians at different times in history.

(1) The idea that the "Kingdom" will come suddenly, through a single-handed divine *fiat*, in a not-so-distant future was wide-spread in the early Christian communities. This eschatological conception in effect implied that Christians would constantly pray that "the figure of this world

may pass away." They would not be concerned at all with the betterment of society, simply because earthly society was destined to an early and catastrophic disappearance. They would consider as unavoidable the ultimate condemnation of the vast majority of mankind and the salvation of only a few. In this perspective even the smallest cell of earthly society, the family, would become a burden; and marriage, though permitted, would not be recommended. The eschatological prayer, "Come, Lord Jesus!" would be understood primarily as the cry of the "remnant," totally helpless in a hostile world and seeking salvation *from* it, not a responsibility *towards* it.

Such an eschatology provides no basis for any Christian mission to society or to culture. It attributes to God alone, acting without any human cooperation, the task of bringing about a New Jerusalem, which would come down ready-made from heaven. It also forgets those New Testament images of the Kingdom which precisely imply cooperation or "synergy": the mustard seed, which grows into a big tree, the yeast which leavens the whole dough, the fields ready for the harvest. An eschatology of withdrawal is, of course, psychologically understandable and even spiritually justified in times when the Christian community is forced to return to itself through external pressure and persecution, as in the first centuries and in more recent times as well; but if transformed into a system, it clearly betrays the biblical message taken as a whole. The "New Jerusalem" is not only a free gift of God coming from heaven, but also the seal and the fulfillment of all the legitimate efforts and aspirations of mankind, transfigured and transformed into a new creation.

(2) The emphasis on human achievement leads to another and opposite extreme: a Pelagianizing and optimistic eschatology based on a belief in the never-ending progress of human society. In strongly maintaining that history has a meaning and goal, this belief in progress—in its capitalistic or Marxist forms—is a post-Christian phenomenon. It is still technically an "eschatology" and has inspired much of modern European and American culture during the past three centuries. In the past decade many Christians have more or

less adopted this eschatology. They identify social progress with "new creation," accepting "history" as a guide towards the "New Jerusalem," and defining the primary Christian task in "secular" categories.

This second eschatology, whether or not it calls itself Christian, takes no account of sin and death, from which mankind cannot be redeemed through its own efforts; and thus it ignores the most real and the most tragic aspect of human existence. It seems to aspire at an unending civilization, ever imprisoned by death, which in fact would be "as horrible as immortality for a man who is prisoner of sickness and old-age."[1] By accepting historical determinism, it renounces the very center of the Christian message: *liberation* from "the powers and principalities" of history through Christ's resurrection and through the prophetic promise of a cosmic transfiguration, brought about by God, and not by man.

(3) The biblical concept of "prophecy" leads us to a third form of eschatology which does justice both to God's power and to man's freedom and responsibility. Prophecy, both in the Old Testament and the New, is neither a simple foretelling of the future nor a declaration of inevitability; it is "either a promise or a menace."[2] In other words, as the Russian religious philosopher Fedotov rightly points out, it is always *conditional*. The "good things" of the future are a promise to the *faithful*, while cataclysms are a menace to the *sinners*. Both, however, are ultimately conditioned by man's freedom. God would refrain from destroying Sodom for the sake of ten faithful, and when the Ninevites repented, he pardoned Nineveh, sparing it from the doom promised by Jonah.

For God is not bound by any natural or historical necessity. Man himself, in his freedom, is to decide whether the coming of Jesus will be a frightful judgment or a joyous marriage feast for him and for his society. No eschatology will be faithful to the Christian message unless it maintains both the power of God over history and the task of man,

---

[1] G. P. Fedotov, *Novy Grad* (New York, 1952), p. 323.

[2] *Ibid.*, p. 327.

which resides in the very real freedom which was restored to him in Jesus Christ for the building of the Kingdom of God.

## II. The legacy of Byzantium

Rome and its imperial tradition exercised an indelible influence, both in the West and in the East, on the way Christians approached all issues involving society and culture. The Christian Church condemned apocalyptic Montanism, with its preaching of withdrawal from history and its negation of culture; but it welcomed the opportunity offered to it by the conversion of Constantine, and in the East even counted him among the saints, "equal to the apostles." This was a clear option taken in favor of assuming responsibility for the whole of the "inhabited earth" (οἰκουμένη). This world was to be influenced not only directly through word and sacrament, but also indirectly through the means which were at the disposal of the State: legislation, administration, and even (more questionably) military force, since now all wars waged against the infidels were seen as holy wars.

There are innumerable legislative texts which illustrate the fact that the Christian empire, without any formal objection on the part of the Church, considered the emperor as a direct appointee of God to rule and protect society. "It is in the name of the Lord Jesus Christ," writes Emperor Justinian (527-565), "that we always start every undertaking and action. For from Him we received full charge of the empire; by Him, we concluded a permanent peace with the Persians; through Him we have dethroned the fiercest and strongest tyrants; through Him, we have overcome numberless difficulties; by Him it has been given to us to defend Africa and reduce it under our power; by Him, to govern [the state] wisely and keep it strongly under our sway... Hence we place our life under His Providence and prepare to organize our armed troops and our officers..."[3]

As is well known, the tradition of Christianized autocracy

[3]*Codex Just.* I, 27, 2.

produced different historical forms in the West and in the
East. The West experienced the fall of Rome in the fifth
century and after having faced the ephemeral attempts of
Carolingians and Ottonians to assume the old Roman imperial power, and after epic struggles by popes to ensure the
Church's independence, it finally recognized in the *Roman
pontiff* a legitimate successor of the Caesars, acknowledging
him as the religious and the political leader of Christendom.
By contrast, in the East the original empire lasted until 1453.
But if this is so, are historians right in assuming that the
system of government accepted by the Byzantine State and
Church was a form of "caesaropapism"? This is a serious
contention. If it were true, it would imply that in the medieval period the Orthodox Church did in fact capitulate to
the "secular," i.e. did accept the second type of eschatology
which sees the Kingdom of God as fully "continuous" with
secular history. In that case Orthodox theology today would
be inconsistent with its own past in criticizing "secularism."

It would certainly be impossible to present here a full
historical discussion of the problem of Church and society
in Byzantium, and I will limit myself to a few brief statements, which could easily be backed with texts and facts:

(1) *Byzantine Christianity never accepted the belief
that the emperor had absolute authority in matters of faith or
ethics.*[4] It could not accept such a belief for the simple and
general reason that it never was a religion of authority. The
ever-recurring theological controversies continued before and
frequently after the meeting of councils called by the emperors to settle them (cf. the triadological controversies after
Nicaea; the christological controversies after Ephesus and
Chalcedon, etc.). Imperial edicts did not stop them. At the
time of the Palaeologan dynasty (1261-1453), each successive emperor was actively pushing the Church towards union
with Rome. The union, however, failed to take place.

(2) *It is not by opposing to the emperors another com-
peting authority (i.e. that of the priesthood) that Byzantine
society avoided caesaropapism, but by referring all authority*

---

[4]I discuss this point at length in my study of "Justinian, the Empire and
the Church," in *Dumbarton Oaks Papers* vol. 22 (1968), pp. 45-60.

*directly to God.* This theocentric view of the universe and of the Church is well expressed in the classic text on the subject, the Sixth Novella of Justinian: "The greatest blessings of mankind are the gifts of God which have been granted us by the mercy on high—the priesthood and the imperial authority. The priesthood ministers to things divine: the imperial authority is set over, and shows diligence in things human; but both proceed from one and the same source, and both adorn the life of man."[5]

In the West this famous text provoked an *institutional* struggle between two legally defined powers, the *sacerdotium* and the *imperium*; but in Byzantium it was understood in a *christological* context. In Christ, the two natures are united, without separation or confusion, into one single *hypostasis*, or person, who is the unique source of their united (though distinct) existence. The adoption of this christological model as a pattern for the organization of society illustrates quite well the contrast between the legally-minded West and the eschatologically oriented East.[6] Indeed, according to Justinian, the common aim of the empire and the priesthood is "a happy concord (ἁρμονία) which will bring forth all good things for mankind," clearly an eschatological goal actually undefinable in legal, political, or social terms.

Of course, Byzantine Christians were aware of the fact that all humans—emperors, patriarchs, priests—would inevitably be in some way unfaithful to the Christian ideal set before them, and thus they never ascribed infallibility to any individual nor even to any legally defined institution. This is precisely why the history of the Byzantine Church offers innumerable examples of highly authoritative voices challenging the arbitrary actions either of emperors or of ecclesiastical authorities. The examples of St. John Chrysostom, St. Maximus the Confessor, St. John of Damascus, and St. Theodore the Studite are well-known. They cannot be considered

[5]Engl. tr. in E. Barker, *Social and Political thought in Byzantium* (Oxford, 1975), p. 75-76.

[6]On the consequences, see F. Dvornik, *Early Christian and Byzantine Political Philosophy. Origins and Background* II (Dumbarton Oaks Studies IX, Washington, D.C., 1966).

as exceptions to the rule, because their writings have been widely read by generations of Byzantine Christians, and were always among the most authoritative patterns of social behavior in the Christian East. None of them, however, challenged either the political system or the *eschatological ideal* defined by Justinian. None of them denied the principle that "divine" and "human" things are inseparable since the Incarnation, and must become "Christ-like," i.e. the "human" must live in "harmony" with the divine. None of them preached either an apocalyptic withdrawal from culture or a separation between the spiritual and the secular which would give "autonomy" to the latter.

How did this ideal manifest itself in practice? There is no doubt that Byzantine society, like medieval western society, made continuous efforts to integrate Christian principles into its legislative texts and its daily practice. This applies to both the State and the Church. "We believe that there is nothing higher and greater that we can do," wrote the emperor Leo III in his *Ecloga*, "than to govern in judgement and justice those who are committed (by God) to our care, to the end that the bonds of all manner of injustice may be loosened, the oppression imposed by force may be set at naught, and the assaults of wrongdoers may be repelled."[7] Similarly, the Church was required, by its canon law, to use its wealth in building and administrating institutions of social welfare.[8] The extent to which both the State and the Church practiced social welfare is wider than one usually imagines,[9] even if the clearly objectionable institutions inherited from pagan antiquity, such as slavery, were only humanized without being fully suppressed.

The overall concern for the *humanum* implied no clear distinction of jurisdiction between the State and the Church; unity of purpose was the very content of the ideal of "harmony" defined by Justinian. This unity of purpose justified the concern and the power of the emperor to administer

[7]Engl. tr. Barker, *op. cit.*, pp. 84-85.

[8]See for example, canons 8 and 10 of the Council of Chalcedon.

[9]See D. J. Constantelos, *Byzantine Philanthropy and Social Welfare* (New Brunswick, N.J., Rutgers University Press: 1968).

practical church affairs (choice of patriarchs, convocation of councils, definition of limits of ecclesiastical jurisdiction, etc.) as well as the participation of church officials in political responsibility. Certainly the canon law of the Church forbade both the appointment of clerics by civil authority (II Nicaea, canon 3) and the assumption of any secular dignity by clerics (Chalcedon, canon 7). But these canons never served as a guarantee against abuses. On the other hand, the Church never considered it an abuse to ensure continuity of the Justinianic "harmony" by buttressing the State in times of need. Thus the "ecumenical patriarch" of Constantinople was, in fact, a political official of the empire, the guarantor of imperial legitimacy; and he would automatically assume the regency of the State when the need for this arose. The roles played either as regents or political leaders by patriarchs Sergius I (610-638), Nicholas Mysticus (901-907, 912-925), Arsenius Autoreianus (1255-1259, 1261-1265), and John Calecas (1334-1347) are examples of this. The typically Byzantine notion of the inseparable union between a universal Church and an ideally universal Empire was also expressed in the very last days of Byzantium. Patriarch Anthony (1389-1390, 1391-1397) was asked by the Great Prince of Moscow Basil I whether the commemoration of the Byzantine emperor's name could be dropped at liturgical services in Russia. "My son," the patriarch answered, "you are wrong in saying: We have a church but no emperor. It is not possible for Christians to have a church and not to have an empire. Church and empire have a great unity and community; nor is it possible for them to be separated from one another."[10]

The Slavs, spiritual children of Byzantium, certainly learned the lesson. The Byzantine pattern of relations between Church and society was faithfully adopted by them with the same ideal of a "harmonious" union in a common allegiance to Christ. Creating their little "Byzantiums" in Preslav, in Ochrid, in Trnovo, in Kiev and in Moscow, Slavic tsars and princes recognized the Church as their cultural inspiration and guide; and the Church assumed this role will-

[10]Engl. tr. in Barker, *op. cit.*, p. 195.

ingly, translating Byzantine texts into the vernacular, and assuming social and political responsibility whenever the need arose. Thus St. Alexis of Moscow became for a time regent of Muscovite Russia (1353-1378), and his example was later followed by Patriarch Filaret (1619-1634). Even the great St. Sergius of Radonezh used his spiritual prestige against the factional feuds of Russian princes.

What then is the legacy of Byzantium to the contemporary Orthodox Church? Theologically, it is primarily in the affirmation that just as man, individually, is destined to "deification" and is fully himself when he is in communion with God, a communion which was realized by Jesus Christ and in Him made accessible to all in the faith, so human society is called to conform itself to God's presence and become the Kingdom of God. The ambiguity of the Byzantine experiment resided, however, on the level of eschatology. Could the Justinianic "harmony," an eschatological ideal, be realized concretely in history? Was Byzantium so fully transformed and transfigured as a society that it found itself in full conformity with God's plan, or was it still a "fallen" society, under the power of evil, sin, and death?

The Byzantine Empire, as a political and cultural entity, never resolved this ambiguity of its claims. The Church, however, always maintained the *distinction* between the priesthood and the empire, between the liturgical, sacramental, and eucharistic anticipation of the Kingdom on the one hand and the empirical life of still-fallen humanity on the other. This polarity between the "already now" and the "not yet" was also constantly proclaimed by the large and prosperous Byzantine monastic movement, whose withdrawal from society and non-conformity to the standards imposed by the empire served constantly as a prophetic reminder that there *cannot* be total "harmony" before the *parousia*, that the Roman Empire is not yet the Kingdom of God, that in order to share in Christ's victory over the world Christians must themselves challenge the laws and the logics of fallen mankind.

## III. Modern times

The survival of Eastern Orthodox Christianity after the fall of Byzantium and of the other Christian empires of the Balkans effectively proves that Orthodox Christians did not believe in the empire as a fully "realized eschatology," but rather—as the monks have always maintained—they discovered the Kingdom in the Eucharist and the personal experience of God, accessible to the members of Christ's body. History itself forced them into recognizing the "other-worldliness" of Christianity, since the "world" had suddenly become hostile again.

The Ottoman Empire, which during four centuries held under its sway the Balkans, Asia Minor, and the Middle East (much of the former Byzantine territories) was a Moslem state, which tolerated the existence of a large Christian population but forbade all Christian mission and made any cultural or intellectual development practically impossible. During all these centuries the Byzantine liturgy, with its rich hymnography, its explicit eschatological character, and its ability to unite the congregation into a real experience of the Body of Christ, became the principal and largely self-sufficient expression of Christianity. Also, following the Byzantine tradition mentioned above, which implied that the patriarch of Constantinople would assume responsibility for society as a whole in the absence of the emperor, the ecumenical patriarch became the *ethnarch*, or civil and religious head of the entire Orthodox Christian population of the Turkish realm by investiture of the Sultan.[11] Thus, while the Church did not actually renounce its mission to society, this mission in practice became limited by the boundaries of a ghetto. This situation, enforced by the tragedy of history, was unfortunately to remain as a habit even when times again became more favorable to mission.

Meanwhile, in Russia a new and powerful Orthodox em-

[11]On the Turkish period, see most conveniently S. Runciman, *The Great Church in Captivity: A Study of the Patriarchate of Constantinople from the Eve of the Turkish Conquest to the Greek War of Independence* (Cambridge, 1968).

pire had taken shape and seemed originally destined to assume the role of a second Byzantium or, if one wishes, a "third Rome." However, the political and social ideas which eventually prevailed in Russia were those of a Western secular state, with Byzantine formulae used mainly to justify autocratic power as such. The ecclesial and canonical corrective which had been acknowledged in Byzantium was lacking. It is in Russia, however, at a time when the empire had not yet taken its final turn towards secular ideals, that a significant theological controversy took place precisely on the social role of the Church. The controversy opposed "Possessors" and "Non-Possessors," two monastic and ecclesiastical groups, equally devoted to the idea of a relevant Christian mission to society but standing for different forms of action and witness.[12] The "Possessors," lead by St. Joseph of Volotsk (1440-1515) found themselves in the tradition of Byzantine theocratic society. They defended the right of the Church, and particularly of the monasteries, to possess great wealth, which was destined to be used for social action: hospitals, schools, and various forms of welfare. This social witness was seen by them as essential to the very nature of Christianity. They were not afraid of the spiritual vulnerability of a rich Church, whose wealth could be used by an inimical State to blackmail it. They believed in the future of a "holy Russia," whose benevolent tsars would support the Church's prosperity and whose ecclesiastical leadership would be forever immune to the temptations of bourgeois comfort, using its wealth only for good works.

The "Non-Possessors," meanwhile, considered that wealth inevitably corrupts, especially that form of wealth which was enjoyed by medieval monasteries: serfs working on immense domains. They saw the mission of the Church primarily as a prophetic witness, pointing to the Kingdom to come. St. Nilus Sorsky (1433-1508), the leader of the "Non-Possessors," inherited the ideals of hesychasm, the mystical and contemplative monasticism of the early Church. He did not trust, as his opponents did, the future of a "holy Russia."

[12]For a brilliant analysis of the controversy see G. P. Fedotov, *The Russian Religious Mind* II (Cambridge, Mass., 1962).

He foresaw its secularization and defended the full independence of the Church from the State.

The controversy ended with the victory of the "Possessors." But the "Non-Possessors" were to be largely vindicated by later historical developments. At the time of the secular Enlightenment the Russian Church was deprived of its lands by Peter the Great and Catherine II. It had no means left for a meaningful social witness. Meanwhile, the spiritual heirs of St. Nilus Sorsky—St. Tikhon of Zadonsk (1724-1783), St. Seraphim of Sarov (1759-1833), the *startsy* of Optino—became the most authentic witnesses to Christian experience in the midst of secular society and succeeded in building bridges between traditional Orthodoxy and the religious revival of the *intelligentsia* in the late nineteenth and the early twentieth centuries.

The past two centuries have witnessed tremendous historical changes in the life of the Orthodox Church. The Ottoman Empire disintegrated; and out of this disintegration new nations, whose religious past is rooted in Orthodoxy, were born. Orthodox Russia, after some hopeful signs of spiritual revival, became the Soviet Union. Millions of Orthodox Christians were dispersed throughout the Western world, where the general frame of reference used in solving "social issues," is determined by Western religious history.

In the midst of this confusion, it was inevitable that the traditional Orthodox values would be severely tested. The new nations in the Balkans, whose cultural identity the Orthodox Church had maintained for centuries of Turkish yoke, had gained their political independence in an atmosphere of secularized Romanticism, which was itself a fruit of the French Revolution. The *nation* itself, not the Christian eschatological and christological ideas, came to be seen as the supreme goal of social action. The Church was frequently unable either to cope with the situation or to discern the spiritual issues at stake. The hierarchs, whose traditional role as "ethnarchs" placed them originally at the forefront of the liberation struggle, soon accepted the comfortable position of obedient civil servants in states led by secularized politicians. Mistaking the new situation for a return to

Byzantine theocracy, they identified the interests of the Church with that of secular nationalism. The Church condemned this identification in an official conciliar statement (1872), labelling it as the heresy of "phyletism"; but the temptation of religious nationalism remains one of the most basic weaknesses of contemporary Orthodoxy. In fact, it represents a capitulation before a subtle form of secularism, which Byzantium with its universal idea of the empire always avoided.

In Orthodox circles today concern for a social witness of Orthodoxy is frequently voiced. Between the two world wars, and also after World War II, a remarkable revival of Christian social activism took place in Greece. It achieved significant results in the field of evangelism but was later criticized—with some justification—for its pietistic and Protestant-inspired orientation. Meanwhile, on the intellectual level, the Orthodox Church attracted to its fold prominent Russian political economists who had previously been Marxists. This pleiad of "religious philosophers," including S. N. Bulgakov, N. S. Berdyaev, S. L. Frank, P. B. Struve and others, began to exercise its influence in the Church itself; and some of them played an important role in Church affairs just prior to the Revolution. Even if some of them, under the influence of an optimistic Hegelianism, adopted a monistic and static philosophy of the universe, usually known as "sophiology" and not unlike the systems of Tillich or Teilhard, their move "from Marxism to Idealism" is a significant event in the history of Orthodox thought. It still fascinates those involved in the renascent religious thought among Soviet intellectual dissidents today.

What attracted these people back to Orthodoxy? Primarily, its eschatological expectation of a transfigured universe; its belief in "deification" as the ultimate destiny of man; its ability, in its liturgical life and in the spiritual experience of its saints, to anticipate the vision of the second coming. They were drawn to Orthodoxy's ability to maintain a "realized" and not only a futuristic eschatology; to speak of the Kingdom of God not only in terms of concepts, or practical achievements, but also as a real vision of the divine presence. These are the aspects of the Orthodox Tradition which make it a living hope not only to intellectuals disappointed in Marxist totalitarian socialism but also to those of us whose destiny is to witness to Orthodoxy in the West.

## Conclusion

Christian tradition cannot be evaluated only in terms of its "successes" and its "failures." As we all know, the New Testament itself does not offer promises of earthly success to the followers of Jesus. Indeed, this must be so, because the true power of Christ will be manifested to the world only on the *last day*, while the *present* power of the Kingdom is fully revealed only to the eyes of faith. Our brief review of the Orthodox Tradition is certainly not a success story; we have only attempted to suggest the main orientations of Orthodox thought and action *historically*. How these historical facts can find their place in a contemporary doctrinal statement must be left to another occasion.

However, a preliminary conclusion can already be drawn: that a Christian solution of social issues is never either absolute or perfect as long as the *parousia* has not taken place, and that an Orthodox Christian can live with that imperfection because he knows that the *parousia* will eventually come; but he cannot be reconciled with imperfection as such. The Orthodox Church has condemned the eschatology of "withdrawal," which would justify indifference and inaction. But—and this is particularly important for our present dialogue—it will certainly never agree that the Kingdom of God present in the Church as Mystery and as an anticipated eschatological reality, is dependent upon the influence which its members may or may not exercise in secular society. Orthodoxy will always maintain that the starting point, the source, and the criterion for solving social issues are found in the uninterrupted, mysterious, and in a sense transcendent communion of the eucharistic gathering.

Historically Orthodox Christians frequently looked for

substitutes for this initial and basic criterion. The Byzantine Empire provided one; nationalism later presented another. But these historical and spiritual mistakes were ultimately recognized as such. They should not, in any case, justify similar substitutions today.